A Staff Officer in
the Peninsula

A Staff Officer in the Peninsula

An Officer of the British
Staff Corps Cavalry During
the Peninsula Campaign of
the Napoleonic Wars

E. W. Buckham

LEONAUR

A Staff Officer in the Peninsula: an Officer of the British Staff Corps Cavalry During the Peninsula Campaign of the Napoleonic Wars
by E. W. Buckham

Published by Leonaur Ltd

Originally published anonymously in 1827 under the title
Personal Narrative of Adventures in the Peninsula

Text in this form © 2007 Leonaur Ltd

ISBN: 978-1-84677-251-1 (hardcover)
ISBN: 978-1-84677-252-8 (softcover)

http://www.leonaur.com

Contents

Publisher's Note

Little is known about E.W. Buckham, the author of this scarce memoir of the experiences of a British staff cavalry officer in Portugal and Spain at the time of the Peninsular War. After his military service it is, according to some sources, probable that Buckham became a clergyman, but we have been unable to verify this.

That he was a man of letters, well educated and proficient in a number of languages—including French, Portuguese, Spanish Greek and Latin with, perhaps, a smattering of Arabic as well—and something of an amateur antiquarian, is evident from his writing. He was also a marvellous observer of people and places who could sketch characters and paint vibrant word pictures in just a few simple sentences.

Buckham is unusual amongst Peninsular War memoirists in that he tells us much about the lives of ordinary people in Portugal and Spain at that time; he describes in detail the hardships and privations, the struggles to make life bearable, as well as the pleasures and irrepressible *joie de vivre* that were a part of life. He also imbues his writing with a great sense of landscape, that adds essential context and texture to other accounts of the Peninsular War.

For this Leonaur edition we have modernised some spellings where the meaning, in context, was ambiguous. We have also excised some footnotes that went into the derivation of place names at considerable length, sometimes in Latin or Greek without translation. These small changes will, we hope, offend no-one.

The Leonaur Editors

Oporto, April 23, 1812

You will doubtless regard the date and place of this letter as an unpardonable outrage upon the unities of sober voyages and travels; since my last from Portsmouth, informing you of being still in that warlike quarter of the land, surrounded by seventy-fours and frigates, post-captains and midshipmen, fresh troops embarking for the theatre of war, and shattered battalions returning from it, was written just seven days ago. The fortnight during which I lingered at Portsmouth, in hourly expectation of receiving an order to embark, was actually an age of torment. Every morning, at the official hour of "nine", I was punctual in my attendance at the Transport Office; there my name was asked with a mortifying regularity, the list duly conned over by a formal clerk, and "no ship assigned you" the invariable reply. At length a convoy was appointed to those vessels which were bound to Portugal, and you may guess my chagrin, when I found that I had now to drag through another fortnight at least, before a second expedition could be ready for sea.

Just at the moment of being made acquainted with this disappointment, I encountered a friend who had arrived in Portsmouth several days after me, and, consequently, ought to have been below me on the Agent's List; he held in his hand an order for a passage, and was then hurrying on board, as the fleet was to put to sea in the evening. There was an apparent unfairness in this proceeding which I could not brook; in a few minutes I was at the door of the Office for Transports, and, upon entrance, found the presiding genius of the place, Captain ——, a bilious looking personage of sixty, walking to and fro in a pair of red morocco slippers. He was alone. I enquired whether any passage had been assigned me to Lisbon? He stopped an instant, surveyed me, and continued his ambulation without uttering a word. At any other time, I should probably have been amused by such imperial conceit, but being then in the worst possible mood for truckling before the insolence of office, I hazarded such a stricture upon the necessity of a little civility and attention on the part of those persons holding Government situations, as immediately kindled the hectic on his cheek; a warm altercation was the consequence, and, not to weary you with a tale already much too long I fear, I left him with the determination of procuring a passage, at my own expense, in some of the merchantmen bound for Portugal. I soon fell in with one destined for this port, made an agreement, and before sunset of the same day bade farewell to Old England.

Were I disposed to be tyrannical, I have it now in my power to inflict upon you an awful account of a hurricane, with all its adjuncts and disastrous consequences; but no—I am resolved to be the first voyager, who having crossed the Bay of Biscay in a gale of wind, has had the uncommon forbearance, in writing to his friends—not to describe.

On the fourth day the land of Portugal was in sight; at the same time the gale abated; the sun shone out with uncommon warmth and splendour, and in a few hours we were close in with the shore. Three of our crew were Portuguese, and one of the three a native of Oporto: to him I paid my court for information. The land we had made was that near Vianna, a town about thirty miles north of Oporto; the prospect was highly rich and picturesque, the rye already changing to a yellow, while the wheat and Indian corn wore a most refreshing green. As we sailed along the shore, the white houses of the inhabitants, studded here and there amidst a scene of verdure, would have produced on any one a happy and pleasing effect. To me, just manumitted from a loathsome crib, it seemed almost enchantment. The sailor Cicerone made me observe, as we glided gently by Vianna, an aqueduct winding beneath a hill, on the top of which was a church called St. Peter's of the Hill (*San Petro d'Outeiro*). In the afternoon, a fishing boat with a large latteen sail, and fraught with a crew of swarthy little devils, came alongside to barter fish for English beef and biscuit. They were but barely decent in their attire, if rags may be dignified by such a name. It is an indescribable kind of sensation which a first view of the inhabitants of a strange country produces. The present sample received from me that sort of scrutiny which people exercise who visit a menagerie, or newly discovered island, for the first time. Their grimaces, rendered more peculiar by black eyes flashing cunning and intelligence—the eagerness with which they endeavoured to drive a good bargain—their varying attitudes—were potent incentives to laughter. Imagine a half naked sun-burnt little fellow, with a cod fish in his hand, shewing him off as a tempting article, with all the airs and graces of a Moorfields broker; another with a turbot; a third with a dog-fish; and these all chattering at once in a strange tongue, and with a vehemence of manner, as if influenced by demoniacal possession.

It was late in the afternoon when we made the mouth of the Duero. The fresh of the river was setting out with a tremendous current. The fort fired signals, intimating that it was impossible to enter the harbour, and a pilot, who came off to us, said we must bring to until morning. Our captain, however, who had some reason for thinking this a mere pretence, in spite of the remonstrances of the consequential little gentleman who claimed a temporary command of the vessel, determined to run the hazard of finding sufficient water on the bar. So soon as the fort perceived our intention, a shot, which nearly carried away our topmast, was fired as a friendly warning that we should desist; and before they could cannonade us again, the good ship was securely riding in the Duero.

My senses were of course wide awake as we moved slowly up the river, and so far was I from preserving the becoming gravity of the traveller, that I am ashamed to confess I betrayed all the thoughtlessness of the schoolboy. We had no sooner dropped anchor, which we. did about two miles up the river, and at the distance of as many from the town, than I prepared to go a-shore; but here I was stopped by the aforesaid consequential pilot, who gave me to understand that I could not be allowed to leave the ship, before the *bizeta*, or customhouse boat, had visited her, which would not be before the following morning. I appealed to the captain, but in vain. In this dilemma I took counsel of my sailor Cicerone, who volunteered to soften his inflexibility with a dollar. This had the desired effect, and in a few minutes I was safely landed.

The night was closing in as I reached the quays in the suburbs of Oporto, and a house inscribed with that intelligible tetragrammaton, *café*, kindly invited me to step within and allay my thirst. The vocabulary was in my pocket, and I presently made mine host understand that I wanted *humcopo de vinho*. It was a tribute due to the great emporium of Tawney, to taste its wine as soon as possible. I quaffed it down with infinite *goût*, tendered my dollar, and received the difference in coins of various description, of which I have yet to learn the value. A man, who was smoking his cigar in the *café*, observing me to look over these with a stranger's eye, told me in tolerable English, that the dollar contained forty *vintins*, and that the wine cost seven. Thanking him for his information, I requested him to mention an hotel to which I might repair for the night. He called to a boy who was loitering on the quay, and directed him to conduct me. Following my dirty guide through a range of narrow alleys, we at length arrived before a large house at the top of a spacious street. The boy, accosting the landlord, pointed me out as *Senor Inglez*, when my host immediately announced himself an Englishman—"Joseph Longstaff, at my service." He informed me he was just making out the bill of a gentleman who was to leave his house next morning for England, and that I should occupy his room. At supper I was introduced to Mr. ——, who was kind enough to say that he would take charge of any letter, and put it into the post-office on his arrival at Plymouth. I readily embraced his offer, and taking to my assistance a bottle of Mr. Longstaff's best priestly port, have consumed one-third of the night over this incoherent epistle.

Oporto, May 10, 1812

Three days ago, I received yours of the 26th ultimo, forwarded to me from Lisbon by the kindness of Mr.——, a gentleman attached to the embassy. Your wish for long letters shall certainly be gratified; that they will prove as entertaining as you are pleased to imagine, I may be permitted to doubt. All I can do will be to send you an account of whatever I turn up in my future rambles; in short, you will continue to receive the same *olla-podrida* kind of epistles which I wrote you when at home—dashed perhaps with somewhat more variety, but in all other respects loose and rambling as ever.

It is a happiness for weak mortals that wonder is a short-lived passion. That titillation of the senses which new scenes produce is certainly delightful, but then we are no longer in the same world with other people. For some eight and forty hours after my arrival in this city, my spirits were in a constant ferment. I saw through half the town before breakfast on the first day of being here, staring and laughing at every thing; in short, I was in such perfect good-humour that nothing came amiss to me.

On the quay-side is the fish-market. Here the women sit in rows frying the dog-fish in rancid oil, surrounded by hungry Gallegos*, who eagerly purchase this *bonne-bouche* as a

---

* Gallego is a name for an inhabitant of Gallicia. These industrious and honest people leave their own country at an early age to gain a livelihood in the cities and large towns of Portugal, where they are employed in the capacity of porters, and in other offices of drudgery.

14

breakfast. The Athenians, you remember, execrated this fish, from an idea they entertained of its feeding upon human flesh; the Portuguese have no such scruples, and will, as the Scotch say, "just take ony thing". The barbers' shops are not distinguished by a pole, as with us, but by a four-pronged block of no ordinary dimensions suspended over the door, intimating to the public their profession as tooth-drawers; while the well scoured brass basin, with a piece cut out to receive the neck, is the identical utensil which served Mambrino for a helmet.

After breakfast I attended high mass in the Church of St. Nicholas. A profusion of tapers were burning before the altar and the pictures of saints which are ranged along the aisles. A band of music ever and anon struck up some delicious notes; the women, shrouded in their *capotas*, occupied the centre, and always continued on their knees; the men stood in the aisles, with the exception of a few near the altar, who were accommodated with chairs; a great many cages with canary-birds were suspended in various parts of the interior, and mingled their loud notes with the sacred melody. A dead silence now ensued; the priest dropped mystical curtesies before the altar, and, at the tinkling of a small bell, an artificial shower of snow descended from the roof, the flakes of which the people intercepted in their fall, and eagerly devoured. This shower was composed of little sugar wafers, and was designed to represent the Host. At first I conceived it was intended to figure out the manna which fell in the wilderness, while the Portuguese themselves seemed no indifferent representation of the hungry Israelites.

I esteem myself fortunate in having landed at this port instead of Lisbon; the head-quarters are at present near Almeida, distant only thirty leagues; from Lisbon, seventy. Having received permission to waste a few weeks in this city previous to joining the Army, I determined, as soon as the fever of curiosity had somewhat abated, to devote a portion of each day to the study of the Portuguese language. Having received from a friend the address of a Professor, I lost no time in paying him a visit. Three pair of stairs in the dirtiest quarter of the town led up to the roosting-place of this sapient gentleman; on entering his apartment, an intolerable odour of fish and oil was almost compelling me to make a precipitate retreat, when I chanced to espy no less a personage than the man of letters himself, engaged in frying *sardinias* (a fish like a sprat), on which he was about to regale. I soon despatched my business; indeed, I do not imagine I could have supported for five minutes the condensed effluvia of the fish, oil, and garlic simmering over a slow charcoal fire in a room about ten feet square.

On the following day, precisely at the appointed hour, he knocked at my door, and so much altered in appearance, that I scarcely believed him to be the same person I had previously seen: his cocked hat was of the most exaggerated description of cocked hats, his hair profusely powdered, his breeches black silk, shoes resplendent with large silver buckles, and a gold-headed cane in his hand—just such a creature, in short, as you meet in Duke's Place on a Saturday. After depositing his watch on the table, not without complimenting himself on his extreme punctuality, he began to read aloud, with a great deal of action, to afford me, as he was pleased to say, some idea of the harmony of the language. Now such words as not, then, are, &c. being in constant recurrence, and these, written *naô, saô, entaô*, being all pronounced, *nông, sông, entông*, you may form some tolerable notion how extremely melodious such a language must be! My mouth has nearly been twisted awry in submitting to half-a-dozen lessons; and then there is a sort of high and low tone to be acquired, which leaves me in despair of ever attaining to proficiency. The language nevertheless has its beauties, a great part of which is comprised in the diminutives, which the people of Oporto, it is said, affect more than any other part of the kingdom. A Portuguese woman who keeps a shop of all sorts not many doors from Longstaff's Hotel, is married to a huge strapping fellow, by name *Señor* Thomas, by whom she has three children. Him she calls *Señor* Thomazino; her eldest girl, Joannina, answers to the appellative Raparega, the second to that of Menina, while the infant is lullabied with such soft words as *coitadinha, povrazita,* &c.

With respect to the society and domestic habits of the people, my acquaintance with them is yet too green to bear me out in hazarding an opinion; as yet I can only speak to what is external The women lead dull moping lives, seldom stir out except to attend mass, and are then so enveloped in their *capotas* that it is difficult to distinguish the better order from the lower. Some, however, have recently adopted a different mode of dressing, and wear straw bonnets and gaudy silk gowns, which become them still less than their native costume. In stature they are rather low, and somewhat inclined to corpulency, for which they are doubtless in a great measure indebted to their sedentary mode of life. Nature, however, by way of compensation for such defects, has kindly bestowed on them melting black eyes, heavy languid eye-lids, and feet almost *a la Chinoise.* The men are not of a description calculated to make a favourable first-sight impression; they appear but very degenerate slips of the Lusitanian stock of other days, and were I not afraid of subjecting myself to the charge of groundless prejudice or premature judgment, I would say, *terra malos homines nunc educat atque Pusillos.*

The convents for both sexes are very numerous, and the streets swarm with monks and friars—friars, white, black and grey, with all their trumpery.

A few days ago, in company with a Portuguese gentleman, I visited a nunnery at Villa Nova on the opposite bank of the Duero. He had a relative here, who was yet in her noviciate; we saw her at the grate, and a most pretty interesting creature she appeared. She said it wanted just four months to her burial, which is the usual expression for taking the veil; at the expiration of which time, mass will be chaunted over her, and she will become dead to the world. In the present instance it was her father's desire that she should take the veil, and he had paid a considerable dowry with her to the convent, which is extremely rich, and admits only the daughters of *fidalgos*, or noblemen. In the chapel there were a few paintings, a degree or two better than what I had hitherto seen, but still pervaded by a most monotonous style of insipid uniformity. Angels being naturally beyond human comprehension, the Portuguese have endeavoured to express the difference which may be supposed to exist between the inhabitants of another world and those of our own, by representing them as much the reverse of themselves as possible. Accordingly they are all excessively florid, with luxuriant flaxen locks curling short about their ears, like the capitals of Ionian columns.

It remains now to give you some account of the society at Longstaff's. You will of course have heard, before this time, of the storming of Badajos. A few days ago several officers arrived here, as well to recruit themselves after their fatigues and dangers, as to dispose of some odd articles of plunder. I have found a very pleasant acquaintance in Captain ——, of the —— regiment, one of the most distinguished in General Picton's division; also with Lieutenant —— of —— regiment. The captain has two or three massy silver chalices, as his hard-earned share of the spoil.

Nothing could withstand the gallantry of our brave fellows. Picton was quite a prodigy. A few hours previous to the assault he was seen hobbling about under a most painful attack of gout or rheumatism; and how he contrived to climb a ladder fifty feet in height, and be among the first on the ramparts, is really most surprising. It is frightful to hear a recital of the many abominations which occurred during the first fury of the sack—it was one wide indiscriminate scene of plundering, butchery, and ravishing. Captain —— told me, that he was induced to enter a house, in consequence of hearing the dreadful shrieks of females; and here he found two soldiers of his own regiment, and a mother and daughter on their knees before them, supplicating for mercy. It was the utmost he could do to prevail on them to leave the house; for all military subordination was dissolved in that uncontrolled licentiousness which is regarded as the just reward of successful valour. Every place which was supposed to contain spirits was speedily broken into, and the scenes which ensued from the fury of the men to possess themselves of this liquid fire, are almost too horrible to gain belief. It was no uncommon sight to find, next morning, two British soldiers lying dead in the streets, pierced through with each other's bayonet, while the keg or bottle, the fatal cause of such mutual massacre, was lying between them.

When the fury of the sack had somewhat abated, and discipline was about to resume its wonted empire, the ludicrous succeeded to the terrible. British soldiers were seen issuing from the gates of the fallen fortress, begirt with all the ample foldings of Spanish *togery*, and bringing away every thing that was either portable or driveable. One fellow had made capture of a calf; the animal refusing to be either led or driven, the Connaught hero, unwilling to relinquish his prize, brought it away in triumph, like another Milo, on his shoulders. It was purchased by the mess-man of the regiment for a bottle of rum!

A few days since, we received an accession to our society, in the person of a strapping young Irish fire-eater, who has come out as a volunteer. He is well furnished with letters of recommendation, and intends *walking* up to head-quarters in a few days, with an oaken cudgel in his hand (which he calls a toothpick) and with a knapsack on his shoulders. He grinds his teeth in agony whenever Badajos is mentioned, cursing his unlucky stars which kept him at home, "when there was so beautiful an opportunity of getting promoted." As he does not know a single word of Portuguese, I was endeavouring to persuade him to remain a few days longer in Oporto, before he commenced his march; but, "Och!" said he, "let me alone for finding my way; the Irish is an universal sort of a tongue."

In my next I will send you some account of this city, having now become familiar with every part of it—Adieu.

Oporto, May 19, 1812

I shall now fulfil the promise of my last, by endeavouring to send you some descriptive account of Oporto.

The city, properly so called, is situated on the declivity of a hill, little more than three miles from the mouth of the Duero. It is the seat of a chancellor, *corregidor*, and bishop, and is one of the seven military governments of Portugal. The present governor is Colonel Trant, an Englishman. In former times it was fortified, of which some vestiges still remain, particularly near the fish-market on the banks of the river, where the old walls and gates are yet in good preservation. The province of Entre Minho & Douro, together with this city, were marked out by Buonaparte, to compose the sovereignty of the King of Etruria, who was to have assumed the title of King of Northern Lusitania— while the provinces of Alentejo and Algarve were destined to reward with a crown the Alcibiades of the day, Manuel Godoy, Prince of Peace. On the east side of the city, towards the residence of the military governor, the houses are built against so steep a part of the declivity which overhangs the stream, that you are forced to climb up to them by steps hewn out of the solid rock. Such situation, however, contributes not a little to its romantic and picturesque appearance; and this part of the city, viewed from a distance, presents a charming *coup-d'œil* with its neighbouring villages, monasteries, and pine-woods.

Oporto may be said to possess but one handsome street, viz. the Rua Nova dos Inglezes, at one end of which is Longstaff's hotel, and at the other the factory house of the wine company, to which every foreigner has access by a proper introduction. Here I was permitted to taste several samples of the primest Duero. One parcel, known by the name of the Duke of York's wine, is the boast of the factory, and prized as a *bonne-bouche* not inferior to the stuff you and I have somewhere read of, which was bottled during the consulship of Opimius, and drunk 200 years after. There is a great difference, however, between the wine you taste here, and that unsophisticated juice which the Portuguese themselves drink. In short, the factory is a laboratory where wine is composed to suit the vitiated tastes of our good people at home. Your citizen, for example, requires a generous roughness; accordingly, the hulls of the grapes are suffered to steep about seventy hours in the must, instead of twenty-four, which the natives deem sufficient. The Greek *bon-vivans*, you know, who were no indifferent arbiters of taste, were in the habit of mixing their wines with a small portion of sea-water, to prevent a determination to the head. The factory, in compliance with our unclassic notions, oblige us with one-fifth of brandy (*agoa-dente*) to produce a contrary effect, thereby shewing themselves an honest exception to most merchants, who generally endeavour to *lower* the strength of their liquors.

Oporto has a number of good streets, not so broad or magnificent as the Rua Nova, but infinitely more agreeable to the pedestrian, inasmuch as they are well shaded by reason of their very narrowness, and contain shops of a pleasing variety. Among these the gold and silversmiths are the most attractive, from their rich display of massy plate and jewels. The workmanship of the former, and the setting of the latter, are for the most part coarse and inartificial;

but the prices are moderate in proportion, and you can purchase plate at a very trifling advance upon its real value. Among the precious stones, the most common is the pale Brazilian topaz, which are exposed for sale in great abundance. These are the only shops which have glass windows; the rest are open to the street.

Towards the west side of the city are two or three irregular sorts of squares, and beyond these, nearly in the suburbs, is a shabby theatre. I was present at a representation a few nights ago. The piece was of Spanish stock reduced into Portuguese idiom, and of which, owing to my scanty knowledge of the language, I could understand little more than the dumb-show. The interior is very gloomy, and the scenic part deplorably mean. The prompter has his post in front of the orchestra, with his head and shoulders screwed into a round box which rises from the front of the stage between the lamps, presenting a sort of cupola in its appearance to the spectators, but open to the actors; from this he *declaims* the piece, in a tone sufficiently loud to be heard in the centre of the pit. The house is badly contrived for distinct hearing from the boxes, and indeed the whole to an Englishman, accustomed to well-lighted theatres, dress circles, and good acting, appears an execrable concern. I must not forget to mention, that the performance was for the benefit of an unfortunate Italian actress, who had recently fallen into the widowhood of her tenth intrigue, with a family of seven children dependent on her professional exertions.

Setting out once more from the Rua Nova, up the banks of the river, you cross by a bridge of boats to a town in appearance not much smaller than Oporto itself. This is Villa Nova; to the westward of which, beneath a hill, are several detached houses forming the market town of Gaya. Here in former times stood Calla or Cale (in the Antonine Itinerary, the last); and Oporto, being afterwards built on the opposite bank, as affording a more convenient station for ships, was called Portus Cale, from which, by a change of letters, Portugal came to be the name of the whole kingdom*. The foundation of Cale is ascribed to the Phoenicians, which may possibly be correct; although I am more inclined to their opinion who think that it was originally founded by the Gauls, and named after them Portus Gallorum. The derivation given for Lusitania is involved in no less obscurity, and after all is a matter of no moment; but as I know your partiality for this kind of research, I send you the following extract, which a good-natured fat friar (named Friar John, and celebrated for playing the best game of billiards in Oporto) was at the pains to transcribe for me.

Lusitania nomen accipit a Luso Liberi patris fllio, et Lysa ejusdem Liberi socio cum Luso Bacchante, unde nunc a Luso Lusitania, nunc a Lysa Lysitania vocatur.

—L. Andreas Resendius.

Part of the foundations of the old town are still discoverable at Gaya.

Returning again up the river towards the Bridge of Boats, the circle of the view is completed on this side by a monastery, built on a high and steep hill which bounds Villa Nova on the eastward. These two towns, Villa Nova and Gaya, are supposed to contain 18,000 inhabitants, chiefly of the lower orders. The current of the Duero is extremely rapid, running at the rate of two miles and a half an hour. It is navigable for twenty-five leagues, as far as Joao de Pesqueira. In Spain I understand it is a gentle stream, its turbulence beginning in Portugal which it enters at Miran-

---

* Isaac Vossius, in his "Observations on the Second Book of Pomponius Mela", derives it from the Callaïci, the present Gallicians. The same author remarks, that in "The Chronicle of the Gothic Kings" in Isidores, it is called Portucula, but in "The Chronicle of Idatius", Portucale. The writers of the middle age universally distinguish between Portugal and Lusitania.

da de Duero the northern boundary of the kingdom, and from this point the current becomes contracted and furious from the rocks which straiten it on both sides. The province of Entre Douro è Minho is esteemed the most fertile of any in Portugal; and *it was* a proverb, that you could not walk a step without hearing the cock crow. According to the Portuguese, however, who always shrug their shoulders, and attribute their poverty to *'los Franceses'*, the Gallic bands were so unnatural as to show no quarter to the high couraged bird, which is their national emblem.

I was present at a fair a day or two ago, which was held at Montezinhos, a little town on the coast, about six miles from Oporto. There seemed to be plenty of good-humour in circulation, but no fire-eaters, no conjurors, no vendors of quack medicines, in short, no *fun;* nor do I think the Portuguese have any word expressive of all that we understand by it. There were some clumsy attempts at dancing, in which the muleteers were the most accomplished performers, having, I suppose, in their intercourse with Spain, become familiar with the steps and attitudes of the *bolero* and *fandango.* Some of the peasant women from the Minho were present, whose broad brimmed hats and particoloured garments formed an agreeable contrast to the mournful *capotas* of the city.

May 21. I have just returned from an excursion to Braga, which I made in company with Mr. ——, a merchant residing at Longstaff's.

The distance from this city to Braga is eight leagues, which we performed very pleasantly in about as many hours. We passed through a charming country, the eye reposing everywhere on a scene of richness. The only disagreeable part of the journey, was being condemned to the back of a tall skittish old mule, surmounted by a saddle peaked before and behind, and having two wooden boxes appended thereto instead of stirrup-irons. On our arrival, we were served at the *Estalage* with a tolerable dinner, for which we were charged, being English, an intolerable price.

Braga is situated in a beautiful and broad valley, well clothed with cork-trees and orange-orchards. It has a cathedral; and a little without the town there is the church monastery of St. Fructuoso. The *Escrivano* of the place, pointed out some few antiquities which he said were the remains of a temple dedicated to Isis, which is very probable, as this was the Augusta Braccarum of the Romans, and we know how prevalent the Egyptian superstition was, both at Rome and its colonies[*].

The Portuguese historian, Manoel Faria de Sousa, has recorded a very delicate and classical inscription found here in his time, which I think you must admire—

Aspice quàm subito marcet quod floruit ante!
Aspice quàm subito quod stetit ante, cadit!—
Nascentes morimur, finisque ab origine pendet,
Ipsaque vita suæ semina mortis habet.

Braga, formerly reckoned as a part of Gallicia, is now the chief town of the Minho, the most industrious and populous province of the kingdom, nearly one-third of the whole population of Portugal being condensed within it. It takes its name of Minho, from the river so called, and which forms a part of the southern boundary of Gallicia. According to history, it derived this name from the great quantity of minium found near its banks. It abounds in fish of various kinds, and discharges itself into the ocean, between the city of Tui and town of Caminha.

As this is probably the last letter you will receive from Oporto, I must tell you what arrangements I have made for

---

[*] The Braccarians were originally a Libyan people, and are said to have migrated into Portugal from the banks of the river Braccada, not far from Cartilage, at a period before any connected history begins.

the march to head-quarters, which are now at Fuente de Guinaldo, a border village in Spain. The trunks I brought with me, I have been obliged to exchange for others of much less dimensions. Mine were preposterously large, and bought under a total ignorance of the nature of Portuguese travelling. I have purchased a Spanish horse for 100 dollars, and two mules, for the best of which I paid nearly eighty pounds, which you may deem almost incredible. It is a he-mule, young, and of carriage size, that is, nearly as tall as a coach-horse in England; and such as these are highly prized and readily bought up. The other cost me twenty pounds, and is somewhat old and vicious. I shall be obliged to leave some of my books behind me, as canteen, bed, and clothes-trunk made a cargo for my best mule, while the other will have enough to do to carry my servant with three days' forage and provisions.

Almeida, June 6, 1812

To my infinite mortification, I am become a fixture in this dismantled garrison, instead of being ordered, as I had hoped, upon field-service. I reached head-quarters at Fuente de Guinaldo on the second instant. My surprise on first entering this village was extreme; though perhaps sufficiently natural to a novice in all military matters. I had certainly prefigured a very different scene. All the flower of the army, I had imagined, would be collected around the hero who commands it—gallant men and stately steeds, in short, all the pomp and circumstance of war within the precincts of a circle! The reality soon chased away the illusion, for the village presented the veriest piece of still-life, not to be quite dead, that I ever saw.

In the marketplace were some half dozen Spanish women, sitting in a row, selling eggs and cabbages, and half a dozen soldiers in their undress were the buyers; now and then an officer in a plain blue coat would cross the plaza, on foot or horse-back; and this was all which met the eye. The place, however, was full, I may say crammed, and had it not been for a friend to whom I brought a letter of introduction, I must have bivouacked for the night; as it was, he gave me up a part of his quarter, which consisted of one room about twelve feet square. Lord Wellington with his personal staff occupied a low-roofed farm-house. The rest of the houses were taken up by officers of the departments of the quarter-master, adjutant, and commissary-generals. These, at the time of my arrival, were all employed in their respective offices, and as every one at headquarters has sufficient employment, the mystery of this apparent desolation soon became intelligible. I received instructions on the following day to station myself at Almeida, and with an "*hei mihi!*" reached my post a few hours afterwards.

It was late in the afternoon of the 24th ult. when I left Oporto. The same evening I reached Penafiel, distant six leagues. The *Juiz de Fora* assigned me a billet on an inn kept by a man of colour, *Señor* Thomas: which is a very convenient way of giving your patron—a name by which the master of the house is always recognized—an opportunity of indemnifying himself for his gratuitous lodging. As the noon-day heat was most oppressive, the most eligible time for travelling is obviously in the morning or evening. My morning, however, was consumed in getting some alterations made in the pack-saddles which pressed unequally on the backs of the mules, and it was night before I arrived at Amaranthe, only four leagues distant from Penafiel.

Here I received a billet upon a convent, and presented it to a friar who was enjoying the cool evening, air at one of its smaller entrances. He directed me to repair to an arched gateway, which, he said, should be opened as soon as the prior had given his sanction. In a few minutes the great gates were drawn back, and another friar with a blazing torch in his hand presented himself as my conductor through a dreary descending passage, from the roof of which the damp was trickling fast, and which led to an inner court where the convent stables were. The time of night, my own loneliness, for my servant had not arrived with the baggage, the gloom of the vault through which we passed, the light, which shone upon the shorn and polished head of the friar, as it streamed from the torch which he held behind him as he guided me along, raised within me a fantastical association of ideas, in which, however, a sense of insecurity had no share.

The Prior soon made his appearance, and gave me a cordial welcome. I thought him, and still think him, to be the only Portuguese gentleman I have met with. Our conversation, owing to my meagre knowledge of the language, would have been very limited, had I not been able to scribble a little bad Latin on my memorandum tables, and to which he replied. In this kind of silent colloquy nearly an hour had glided on, when a waiting friar announced the supper. The fraternity had taken their repast before I arrived, and the greater part had already retired to their cells. Descending to the refectory, I was presented with water in a silver basin, which custom, previous to sitting down to table, is universal in all good families. A civet of hare, roast partridges, and old wine were duly appreciated, you may be sure, after a sufficiently long fast. The bed and bed-room assigned me were the same which Marshal Soult had occupied the night previous to his attack on Oporto.

In the morning I found in readiness a regular English breakfast, *viz.* tea, coffee, with eggs and cold meat. After this, the Prior was obliging enough to shew me over the convent. The founder of this religious house was St. Domingos. The corridors and dormitories are spacious, and, though of no order in architecture, are pleasing and striking. The church, in its exterior view, is disfigured by a conical dome roofed with tiles of a bright-red colour, and which gives to the whole a sort of oriental appearance. The convent library is very indifferent. Soult, who is a bibliomaniac as well as Junot, had despoiled it of its most valuable books. The only ones which I saw worth coveting were a splendid History of St. Domingos, the founder, and the works of one Jerome Ossona, a learned prelate of the sixteenth century, who is proudly designated the Portuguese Cicero. Besides being a very great theologian, he was so good a patriot, that when the death of his sovereign, Sebastian*, and the total overthrow of his army by the Moors at the battle of Alcasar, was announced as he was giving a lecture to the students of Coimbra University, like Eli the judge of Israel, he fell backwards and immediately expired.

The town of Amaranthe is on the banks of a beautiful stream, called the Tamega; which is crossed by a remarkably neat bridge within sight of the convent gate. It has derived its name of Amaranthe from the Lamarantini, who were anciently settled here. Previously to quitting the convent, I paid a visit to the kitchen, where such substantial preparations were going forward as fully asserted the claim of its hospitable inmates to the title of *bons vivans*. Through the centre of the kitchen flowed a stream of water, grated at both ends, in which some fine carp were enjoying themselves during the short time they had to live. The cooks were all friars of subordinate degree, and the effect of seeing these unshod sons of St. Domingos go through the manual exercise of the culinary art, was irresistibly comic.

As I mounted my horse, the waiting friar above mentioned stood at the portal and softly ejaculated *"Pel' amor de Deos!"* The hint was necessary, as I should never have presumed to insult the dignity of the order by depositing my mite with one of the meanest of its sons. I slipped a dollar into the friar's hand, received a flood of benedictions, and rode forwards.

The country between Amaranthe and Lamego was really enchanting; oranges and lemons were in many places overhanging the road. At Mezamfrio I halted an hour during the noon-tide heat, and found for the first time

---

* Sebastian and his fine heroic army perished in a headstrong and ill-concerted expedition against the Moors in Africa, about the year 1568.

distinctive marks of an invading army. Descending towards the Duero by a road surrounded on every side with vineyards, after a league of sunny travelling, I passed the river and reached Lamego. Here I found part of a British division quartered. It was also a hospital station, which rendered it a difficult matter to obtain a billet. From the splendour of the address which appeared on the one I received from the *Juiz de Fora, viz.* "Ao Illmo Senr," &c. I drew a good omen; but such a house, such an *illustrious* Señor, such a garret assigned me for a quarter, as will cure me of having faith hereafter in any but worst auguries! Here, for the first time, I essayed the softness of my travelling bed, as my *illustrious* patron either would not, or could not, accommodate me with one.

The next morning, when anxious in the extreme to proceed onwards, I had to encounter a cruel disappointment—my horse was lame; and I had time, more than enough, during two days of unpleasant detention, to visit every corner of the town. Lamego (Lamecum) is one of the most ancient cities of Portugal, and the seat of a bishop -who resides here. In this city it was that the king Alphonzo Henrique, son of the Duke of Burgundy, and so famous in history for the signal victory he obtained over five Moorish kings at the battle of Ourique, held the famous assembly of the states at which the succession was settled in his family. The city is surrounded on every side by mountains, and silver mines were formerly worked in its neighbourhood[*].

The remainder of the route to head-quarters lay through a barren and ruined country. This part of the province of Beira, naturally infertile, has been subject to all the ravages

---

[*] "The Antiquities of Lamego" were written and published by Roderic Perez *circa annum* MDXXXVI, a work very highly extolled by Roderic de Cunha in his "Historia dos Arcebispos de Lisboa", but which I have never been able to obtain.

of war. A thin and squalid population, houses in ruins, fields under no culture, presented on every side a mournful uniformity of misery. In some places through which I passed, not a bit of bread was to be obtained. One night, near to Moimenta de Beira, I took up quarters in an *estalage*. The only room in it was a long chamber, like a coach-maker's loft, built over the stables. The wretched-looking inhabitants were huddling round a few embers at one extremity, and simmering some oil and water in an earthen pot, which, poured over some slices of Indian corn bread, composed their supper.

With great difficulty and not without producing some *pizettas*, I procured a morsel of dried salt fish, which goes under the general name of *bacalhao*. Corn for the cattle I had with me, and the inn afforded Indian straw. At dusk a brigade of mules arrived, and shortly afterwards, eight or ten wild, strapping muleteers ascended the loft, and began arranging their beds for the night. They are always well supplied with blankets, which they require in the daytime for their mules, and a straw pack-saddle is ever at hand for a pillow. The host and his family now stretched themselves on the floor before the embers, the muleteers soon began a nasal concert in the middle, while myself and servant had our cribs at the farther end of the apartment. Sleep was out of the question; the snoring sons of labour above, the uneasy and contentious beasts below, were greater foes to sleep than ever Macbeth was, and methought the day seemed never yet so slow in breaking.

On the following day, passing through Pinhel, another sombre town, I descended upon the Coa by a wild and mountainous track, and after a short ascent on the other bank, had the fortress of Almeida before me, distant one league from the river, and six leagues from the town I have just mentioned. As I approached the ditches of the ramparts I could not but be surprised and amused with the number and largeness of the lizards, which were gambolling in the sunshine just like so many playful kittens, while some of them were certainly not less in size. Had the age of philters not gone by, methinks there were sufficient here to charm all the world, nor could the most arrant witch of Thessaly have desired sleeker or plumper animals. At the gate of the fortress I was stopped by the officer of the guard with the usual formalities, and two soldiers were sent to escort me to the governor. Passing through an ante-room where some orderlies were in waiting, I knocked at the door of the Governor's closet, entered, and began giving some account of myself in execrable Portuguese, when observing him smile, I broke out with a "Pray do you speak English?"

" I have the honor to be an Englishman," was the reply "and shall be extremely happy if you will dine with me today."

The Governor is Colonel Le Mesurier, and being dressed in Portuguese uniform, while the garrison itself displayed none but native troops, my mistake was not so inexcusable. At dinner I met Don Julian Sanchez, the guerrilla chieftain, a fine, well whiskered looking soldier: *"O! si sic omnes."*

Here I had an opportunity of comparing the two languages as far as regards the *sound,* being content to catch a tithe of the *sense.* There were at table several officers of distinguished rank, as well Portuguese as Spanish. In hearing the language of the first spoken without understanding what is said, the temptation to laugh is irresistible—at least I found it so. Not so with the Spanish, which is grand and sonorous, and seems to confer an elevation of character upon the speaker. A Portuguese, besides his grimaces and high and low tones, is dilatory and even drawling in his speech; the Spaniard prompt, energetic, and precise.

We have a courier attached to the garrison, who takes on the letters to Celorico, where he meets the post from head-quarters to Lisbon. I shall send this under cover to my friend ———, and request it may be forwarded by the first trader or transport, as being too bulky for the regular conveyance.

Almeida, July 30,1812

My life is now but a stupid chronicle of breakfasts, and dinners, and sleep. I cannot express half the vexation I feel at being immured in this vile garrison, while our troops, by all accounts, are in full march upon Madrid.

The news of the battle on the 21st instant, fought near Aripeles, in the neighbourhood of Salamanca, will have reached you before this arrives. All that we know at present is, that a glorious victory has crowned our arms, and that Marmont was carried off wounded from the field. The Lisbon mail of to-morrow will bring us the Portuguese account; but it is to the London papers we must look for a detail.

The French prisoners are pouring down upon us. The Spaniards have treated them, by all accounts, with a most revolting cruelty during the march from Salamanca, and the joy of the poor fellows was unbounded when they were delivered into the custody of the Portuguese. A French officer told me, and I had it confirmed in various ways, that if any of the prisoners through fatigue lagged behind in the route, they were immediately bayoneted. This spirit of retaliation is the damning spot of the Peninsular warfare. The lives of ten thousand, or twice ten thousand lost in a hard-fought field, excites not half the emotion which the mind feels at the cold-blooded massacre of a few defenceless beings.

The "war to the knife" which the Spaniards have proclaimed, is of the same character with that of the tomahawk and scalping knife of the savage. In several proclamations of the supreme junta, which were published in 1810-11, the knife is particularly recommended as a proper instrument in the extermination of the French, and is classed among the *"armas blancas"*—such as swords and bayonets; and, in the account of an insurrection of some of the inhabitants of Madrid against the French troops in 1808, the success of the Spaniards is ascribed mainly to their adroit use of this weapon. The Spaniards withstood the enemy— *"sin mas annas que las navajas embotadas de picar tobaco."*

Owing to the kindness of the gallant governor of this garrison, in giving me free access to any books or documents in his possession, which may enable me to form a right judgment as to the character of the war, I have devoted a good deal of leisure to the perusal of political pamphlets and manifestoes circulated during the first stages of this momentous struggle. Though the greater part of these contains much violent ebullition of patriotic sentiment, yet it is evident, from their own confessions, that they were addressed to a people far from being cordial or united in the great cause of freedom. Since that period they are more than ever reconciled to the yoke, and whether at last they will be roused to stand forward as men, or prefer being handed down to posterity as slaves, the present advance of our army into the interior will afford an opportunity of determining.

I must now give you some little account of this garrison. More than two-thirds of the town is in ruins, and the houses which do remain afford little more than bare shelter. In the one which I occupy, I am indebted to some tarpaulins as a security from the rain, and which has, in spite of all precautions, more than once over-flooded me. Massena opened his trenches against this fortress on the 15th of August 1810. On the 26th, eleven batteries commenced their destructive fire. The garrison consisted of 5000 men. On the 27th the large powder magazine in the citadel blew up with terrific explosion. Half the artillery, and a great many of the inhabitants, who had there sought shelter from the shot and shells, perished. Massena, upon the reduction of this important fortress, advanced into Portugal, Lord Wellington retiring before him on the Coimbra road.

There is no society here but that of the Portuguese officers, which is very so-so. In English, we muster as follows—the governor, an officer of the medical department, and three of the commissariat. The present garrison consists of two Portuguese regiments and some dismounted cavalry. About the middle of last month a very fine regiment, the 7th Cacadores, marched through, and in which were several British officers. Their situation, however, seems far from being an enviable one; the manners and habits of the Portuguese being so opposite to ours that little friendly association can subsist between the two. They have no common mess, and their only general meeting is that which takes place on parade.

The *esprit de corps*, therefore, which confers such a marked character upon British regiments, must not be expected here, and the only conceivable bond of union must arise from the consciousness of their being embarked in a common cause, wherein they are resolved to do their duty; but to the private relations and friendly sympathies, which ought to subsist between fellow-men encountering the same dangers, they seem completely estranged.

The Portuguese, however, are not without their virtues; they are grateful, both for the real assistance we have afforded them, and for the knowledge they have acquired from us as to the movement of armies, and indeed of the whole routine of military tactics. The docility with which they have submitted to be taught, cannot too highly be commended; and had the Spaniards been of the same humble mind, they would have presented a respectable army in the field, instead of a band of ragamuffins.

It is entirely to Marshal Beresford that the Portuguese are indebted for being what they are. He has been to them what the Count de Lippe was in former times, the creator of a regular army out of a heap of confusion. To effect this he was compelled to have recourse to measures of severity, which shocked at first the pride of the nation. The command of regiments had generally been reserved for those of noble families, without any regard to their military talents. Boys, and even infants, as sons of *fidalgos*, were gazetted to various ranks. The attention of their new leader was soon called to such abuses; and some of Lord Beresford's early general orders contain such notices as these—"Illmo. Señor ——, Major of ——, is superseded in his command, not being able to write his name"—"Illmo. Señor ——, *Capitao* of ——, is also superseded, having been seen embracing a common soldier, to the subversion of military discipline", &c.

I picked up an anecdote the other day, which I thought laughable. It was at the Governor's table, on the feast of St. Anthony, the patron saint of the Portuguese—When the people of this nation threw off the Spanish yoke, the entire success of the enterprise was attributed to the plenary protection of St. Anthony; and the new king (John IV.) was compelled to declare his saintship *generalissimo* of his armies. The monarch, they say, blushed to countenance the superstition, but was obliged to meet the wishes of an enthusiastic people who had just presented him with, a crown. The bust of the. saint was accordingly carried in solemn procession; and being placed at the head of the army; was, with a most unexampled celerity of promotion, endued successively with the uniforms and insignia of the various grades. He was first made Corporal St.

Anthony, Serjeant St. Anthony, *Capitao* St. Anthony, and then *Generalissimo* St. Anthony. The bust was always carried at the head of the troops. All orders were issued in his name. But, alas! in the first *rencontre* with the enemy in the neighbourhood of Sabugal, a fatal shot carried away St. Anthony's head! Universal terror immediately pervaded the ranks, and the simple Portuguese paid for their superstition at the price of a total defeat.

The country round Almeida is one uniformly arid and rocky plain, extending, with little variety or relief, as far as the eye can reach, except on the side towards the Coa and on that towards the north, where the prospect is bounded by the dismantled town of Castel Rodorigo, built on a hill, and distant three leagues from the garrison. The first Spanish town of any note is Ciudad Rodorigo, distant six leagues; and the nearest village is that of Aldea de l'Obispo*.

The contiguity of two rival people, one would have thought, arguing from the natural love of superiority in mankind, must have given birth to emulation and industry on either side; but the advantage is altogether with the Spaniard. A running stream forms the boundary of the two countries. On the Portuguese bank is the wretched village of Val-de-la-Mula, inhabited by a few squalid beings; on the opposite shore, and at the distance of a mile, is the wealthy and populous village of Aldea. Here the farm-houses are excellent, the church well kept, and the inhabitants totally differing both in features and costume.

A few evenings ago I rode over to the said Aldea, for the purpose of purchasing some wheat-straw, which the Spaniards chop very small, and give to their cattle as forage. As it was Sunday, and a saint's day to boot, such a propitious conjunction could not be allowed to pass without some more than wonted festivity.

---

* Aldea de l'Obispo, "Village of the Bishop".

Upon arriving at the village-green, I found two rustic senoras and their partners, who were moving in the lazy mazes of the *fandango*, accompanied by *castanets*. The village damsels were arranged on one side of a square, and before them stood the Orpheus of the place, bandy-legged, and lame like the great Tyrtæus, and attired in the usual costume of slouch hat and chocolate-coloured vest. He sung and played at the same time.

His only instrument was a kind of wooden drum, like a *tambourin*, but square, and apparently solid, though hollow and filled with something which increased the sound. This instrument is probably some remains of the Egyptian *sistrum*, which was usually embellished, if I recollect, with the figure of a cat. Even this device the Spaniards might assume with a local propriety; for the Sierra de Gata (Cat Mountains) are in this neighbourhood. At a little distance from this festive group were a number of Spaniards, mostly aged, who seemed as intent on the dance as though they had been solving a problem. After taking chocolate with the *Señor Padre* (the priest), I returned to Almeida just as the gates were closing for the night.

St. Pedro de Rio Seco, November 15, 1812

The disastrous turn which our affairs have taken must already, in part, be known in England. Bad news is a quick traveller. Fourteen days ago, and had any one hinted the probability of a retreat, he would have been regarded as one whose untoward nature it was to draw the worst auguries from the fairest prospects. Nay, had it rained stones, or had an ox spoken from the governor's window, the portent would never have disturbed our confidence.

On the 1st instant I had gone over to Pinhel, a neighbouring town, to be present at the annual fair. On the following day a courier arrived, bringing me a note from the governor, countermanding some commissions, and concluding with—"Head-quarters are at Valladolid, and our army in full retreat." I lost no time in returning to Almeida, anxious to learn what I could of the true state of affairs.

On the 3rd, a letter was received from headquarters, then at Rueda, desiring that arrangements should be immediately made by the governor and commissariat for the reception of 6000 sick. About the 7th they began to pour down in great numbers, having been hurried off from the hospitals in Valladolid and Salamanca as fast as transport could be collected. This village of St. Pedro, distant four miles

Note from the original edition: the Letters between July 30th and November 15th contained nothing worth transcribing.

from Almeida, and possessing a large church, was soon fixed upon as the most convenient place for a temporary hospital. I took up my residence here on the 6th. The greatest part of the village being in ruins, there was little to choose among the habitations which were standing—all being equally wretched. At length I found one which afforded a small room detached from the family apartment, and which now serves as salon, office, and bed-chamber.

A great number of the medical and purveyor's department arrived on the following day, and before night the church was nearly filled with the sick and wounded. Next day it became literally crammed full, as every hour brought in a considerable arrival. From daybreak to dusk I am incessantly engaged in attending to the applications of officers in charge of parties, and requiring transport, provisions, or other assistance.

When the fatigues of the day are over, Staff-surgeon K——, and Mr. ——, one of the purveyors, are my regular guests at dinner, when we solace ourselves with gin-twist and cigars. Our viands are not of a very costly description, nor of any extensive variety. Each day sees the table spread with a wooden bowl of rice-soup and a lump of tough beef; but we eat it with thankfulness, and never fail to recollect what a sweet morsel such a piece would have been to many a poor fellow during the retreat.

K—— is a German, exceedingly tall and spare in his person, extravagantly fond of his pipe, which he calls his "wife", and possessed of a vast fund of humorous anecdotes. A few nights ago, as we were sitting in triumvirate conviviality, a soldier entered to say that a lady was without, desirous of seeing me. The night was dark, and the rain descending in torrents, when, in a lane at no great distance from my quarters, I found a cavalcade consisting of a female on horseback, another on a mule with an infant in her arms, and a batman leading a baggage animal. One of the females addressed me with an unnecessary apology, and stated herself to be the wife of Staff-surgeon ———. She had been travelling since break of day without knowing whither; her husband, who was on duty, having failed to overtake her on the road. She was drenched with rain and nearly famished; the whole party having had nothing but two biscuits amongst them during the day. I conducted them to my billet, where the miserable fire of the inhabitants was soon kindled into a flame, and fed from time to time with hay and straw; for of wood there was none but what was too green for prompt burning. While they were drying their dripping garments, my servant was all alacrity in preparing some fried collops; and honest K———, forsaking his pipe, insisted on being allowed to stand cook for the infant. There was plenty of white bread and goats'-milk in the house, which the culinary skill of the doctor soon converted into excellent pap.

While this was going forward, I went in search of the *Juiz*, to endeavour to procure them a quarter for the night. This was no easy matter, every place being full, and the night so advanced that the doors of every house were closed. At length we discovered one occupied by a corporal and four men belonging to an escort, who were content to relinquish their room and fire, upon my engaging to send them a canteen of rum to assist them in wearing away the night in an adjoining shed.

I can scarcely describe one half of what I have seen and felt during my residence in this village. Imagine to yourself the sufferings of the poor sick and wounded fellows dragged along in open bullock-carts, under an almost incessant rain; some of them with their wounds festering from want of being dressed, and all nearly famished with hunger. A great many died in the carts, and a still greater number, unable to endure the tortures of being dragged along over roads so rugged, crept out and died by the wayside. One would naturally suppose, that scenes like these would soften the minds of the sufferers into a mutual sympathy and tender desire of imparting relief, as far as they had the ability; but from what I saw myself, and heard from others, very little of this generous feeling existed; while some, urged on by pain and hunger, evinced a ferocity of nature at the thoughts of which humanity sickens. It is fearful to think that the pangs of death were rendered more bitter to many by the eager contention of the survivors to become possessed of any little article of property which the expiring sufferer might have about him, such as a shirt, handkerchief, or a piece of biscuit. In some instances death was accelerated to obtain them.

K—— told me of a circumstance which came under his own observation. A poor fellow was lying in the hospital at this place, whose leg had been amputated. A mortification ensued, and many hours could not have elapsed before death, in its natural course, must have put a period to his misery. It was in the morning when K—— told the sufferer that he could not survive twenty-four hours. Visiting the hospitals towards evening, he was surprised at not discovering his patient; and upon making enquiry from the attendants, was informed they had just buried him. Suspecting some foul play, he had the body taken up, and discovered such marks of violence about the throat as fully confirmed his suspicions. A few dollars which this unfortunate man was known to possess, had led some of his comrades to the perpetration of this atrocity, but who the miscreants were could never be discovered. They themselves probably survived not many days; for the mortality was a raging one. As soon as night sets in, the wolves, which are numerous in this part, prowl about in droves, and quickly remove the bodies from the shallow graves which are hastily scooped out to receive them.

Almeida, November 26,1812

I had no time to finish my letter at Rio Seco; it bears indeed but too many marks of the haste in which it was written, and I fear you will be puzzled to decipher it. I returned hither on the 19th, the hospital having been cleared as expeditiously as possible, under the impression that the French would pursue us into Portugal.

Arriving once more at my old quarters, I learnt that the governor had set off that morning for Ciudad Rodorigo to see Lord Wellington. The report was current that the French would continue to follow us up, but on the following day it became understood that they were retiring upon Salamanca, and immediately our troops began to move off into winter cantonments. Two or three days after this, I received orders to station myself at Villa Torpine, a village about two leagues from the garrison, for the purpose of superintending the supply of the Spanish army, which was to move by divisions through that place, on their way to Gallicia. Fifty bullock-carts laden with biscuit had already arrived there; but to procure either meat or spirits was impossible. On ordering the biscuit to be deposited in the church, the greater part was discovered to be in a heated state; a circumstance not to be wondered at, since it had been brought up from the Duero in open carts, and exposed, during the six days of passage, to an incessant rain.

The first division of the Spanish army arrived shortly afterwards, and were loud in their complaints when they found such miserable entertainment. I permitted their commissaries to select the best of the biscuit, hoping that a fresh supply would arrive before the second division marched in; in this, however, I was disappointed. The troops bivouacked in the streets, as the houses could scarcely contain all the officers of the staff. Large fires were kindled immediately, and every shed, found empty, pulled down for the purpose of converting its timber into fuel. I was amused with the Spaniards' mode of messing. The biscuit allowed to a mess is put into a cauldron of water, vegetables of any kind, cabbage, onions, garlic, nay even thistles being added. When sufficiently boiled, the mess is summoned by a sergeant, and consists of fifteen or sixteen exclusive of two or three women and children. The women being allowed but half the rations which a man receives and a child but one fourth part, the distribution is effected in the following equitable manner— they all form a circle round the cauldron, each furnished with a tin pot and spoon. At the first signal the men advance, and take out a spoonful. At the second, the men and women advance together. At the third, the men only. At the fourth, men, women, and children; and they go on in this order until the whole is eaten up.

On the following day, the second division arrived, and the biscuit having become so hot that you could scarcely bear your hand on the heap, the troops, headed by their officers, broke out into an open riot, forced their way into the church, and proceeded to plunder all before them. So infuriated did they seem, that I became at length compelled to effect my escape by the window, as all remonstrances on my part were met with clamour and insult. I repaired to the Spanish general's quarter, and reported the circumstance. He received my representation by telling me very coolly that we should have provided them with better entertainment.

As I had now nothing more to do at Villa Torpine, I sent my report to head-quarters, and returned to Almeida. Upon arrival, I had the pleasure of meeting with Captain ———, my early acquaintance at Oporto. I gave him the best shake-down my poor quarters could afford, and received an ample return in hearing from him a recital of that part of the retreat which fell under his observation.

Had the Spaniards been at all hearty in the cause the retreat from Burgos would never have happened; but the truth seems to be, that they will neither themselves resist the French nor assist us in fighting their own battles. The enthusiasm which the Madrilenos, and the inhabitants of other great towns which our troops entered, evinced, was of a very doubtful character. To those who looked farther than the surface, it was evident that there existed a general indifference as to whether the French were driven out of Spain or not. A great part of the nation regard the contest as one between France and ourselves; "We are compelled", say they, "to fight them somewhere, and the Peninsula is as good a theatre for war as the soil of any other country." By this view of the case, which perhaps may have some truth in it, all considerations of gratitude become of course ex-cluded. To assist us is only, they think, to prolong the con-test to their own prejudice; and though perhaps they would be well pleased to be rid of the French altogether, yet so lightly does slavery hang about them, that they consider their redemption as not worth the price they must pay to obtain it. In short, you may say to a Spaniard what a Greek master was accustomed to say to a manumitted slave who had abused his freedom—"Be a slave, since thou knowest not how to be free."

Although our troops suffered much during the retreat, yet upon the whole it may be regarded as a very masterly performance, and calculated to throw a lustre upon him who is the life-blood of the cause, less dazzling indeed, but more solid perhaps than what attends on victory itself.

The enemy's cavalry were more than twice the number of our own; and with all the ardour of their national character superadded to that which pursuit itself inspires, hovered upon the march, and harassed it unceasingly. Much of the privation which our men suffered, with regard to provisions, was attributable to this cause; although much, no doubt, was owing to a want of subordination, which is so difficult to preserve in a retreating army. The depots on the line of march would have been fully adequate to any fair demand could due methods have been found to effect the distribution of the supplies; but while the incessant annoyance of the enemy rendered the transport of provisions difficult to accomplish, the troops themselves were so little subject to strict discipline that so long as they could shoot pigs, or break into wine-cellars, they would not bestow a little pains in procuring provisions through the regular channel.

On the plains of the Aripeles, it was Lord Wellington's design to draw the French into an engagement, when another signal victory would doubtless have swelled retreat into triumph. But the enemy shewed no disposition to meet us again on that proud field. Captain —— was one of the last of ours in Salamanca, and which he left just as the French were entering by the opposite gate. Previous to his departure, he witnessed a humorous instance of political tergiversation. The keeper of a coffee-house in the Plaza, upon our first entrance in the summer, displayed over his door a board, notifying *"Cafe pour les Officiers Francois."* As such an inscription was no longer available to mine host when we had become masters of the city, and was at the same time no pleasant memento of the colour of his patriotism, he, with a presentiment of its future utility, turned the offensive side to the wall, while a painter was employed to depict on the other the novel intimation of "Good English Coffee House."

Señor Bonifacio was in the act of restoring the signboard to its original reading as my

Friend —— was leaving the square.

"Exuno disce omnes." Next summer I hope to hear of the tables being turned again.

Vizeu, December 10, 1812

The day after my last letter was despatched to you from Almeida, I received orders to accompany Deputy Commissary General ——, on a tour of inspection which he was about to make through the cantonments of the army.

On the evening of the 29th ultimo, we set forward from Almeida on our journey, and with some difficulty obtained shelter for the night in the ruined village of Carvilhal, distant about three leagues from the passage of the Coa. This was indeed a place of wretchedness and desolation. The houses were all either roofless, or rendered otherwise untenantable by being stripped of their doors and window-frames, which had been burnt for fuel. In one of the hovels into which we peeped, allured by a little light proceeding from a decaying fire, we discovered four of our soldiers lying dead around the hearth, while a fifth was just expiring in a corner. They were of the number of those who had been hurried down from the Spanish hospitals.

The Portuguese inhabitants did not exceed a dozen in number, and one of them, who officiated as a *Juiz*, shewed us to a stable, where we prepared for passing the night, by kindling a fire, and spreading our bear-skins as near it as possible; the servants, horses, and mules occupying the rest of the interior. I slept as soundly as though reposed on down, notwithstanding the squealing and kicking of our long-eared beasts, and the lengthened *arris** or curses of the muleteers. It is honest Sancho, I believe, who exclaims, "Blessings upon sleep, for it covers a man all over like a cloak."

We rose early and continued our route upon Celorico. As we advanced, the appearance of the country began to improve. The track of war however was still but too visible. Numbers of carts laden with sick and wounded, and followed by crowds of half-famishing women and children, were slowly moving on by the same route with ourselves. The Sierra Estrella mountains began to rise in majesty before us as we advanced, and the villages to put on a more smiling appearance.

At Peña Cova, considered half-way between Almeida and Celorico, we stopped to refresh at an excellent house belonging to the curate of the parish, a hospitable and benevolent character. He has been extremely kind in his attention to the sick who have passed this way, and his housekeeper, who seems to be made of sterner stuff than her master, complained of his having given away nearly all the grapes and apples which had been laid in for winter-stock.

We now crossed the Mondego, and it was late in the afternoon when we reached Celorico, and nearly nightfall before a billet could be obtained, as every house in the town was literally crammed with British officers.

On the 3rd of December we again set forward. The season was as mild as you have it in May, and the country as we advanced seemed to put on some new feature of beauty. The Estrella, snow-capped and mingling with the clouds on our left, the ridge of Busacos in front, while the Vizeu and Tormes mountains enclosed us on the right. Numerous flocks of sheep, with fleeces rivalling those of the Merino

---

*The execration which the muleteers of Spain and Portugal use to drive on their beasts, or to scold them for misdemeanour.

breed, were seen pasturing in the fertile vales beneath the Estrella, and up the mountain sides as far as the eye could reach. From the countless streams which descend from these lofty mountains, the pasturage is of course extremely luxuriant. The first village after leaving Celorico is Cortico, and a mile or two farther Villa Cortes, from which you have Coral in view, and on the left Linhares, deeply embosomed in the Sierra.

We next came upon St. Payo, a pretty romantic place, situate on the banks of the river Mello, having a good stone bridge, and the best built church which I have seen for a long time. The 12th Light Dragoons were quartered in this and some adjacent villages, which all abound in forage. Continuing our route, we passed near Govea on the left, in appearance a handsome town. Some years ago an Englishman established a cotton manufactory in this place, when, after he had sufficiently benefited the country by a disclosure of his art, the Portuguese, with Christian gratitude, cut his throat. A splendid looking convent for men stands a little without the town. The cowled generation are but few at present, and the greater part of the edifice serves as an hospital for our sick.

We put up for the night at Vinho, and had quarters assigned us in a priory, where I had considerable entertainment in ransacking an old library of histories and antiquities. In this place there is a convent for women; a particularly neat edifice built on the banks of a little river.

On the following day's march we closed in with the base of the Estrella range. Arriving at Penanzes, where we fell in with the high road which crosses the Sierra to Castello Branco, nothing could exceed the beauty of the scene. The eye wanders on every side over innumerable villages. From one point we had in distinct view the villages of St. Passar, Sta. Mariana, St. Martinha, St. Jago, Sta. Comba, and Gea-on-the-hill. We struck out of the high road, and bent our course towards the last-mentioned place, for the purpose of making some arrangements with General Clinton, who was quartered there. The route to this village is truly delightful. You ascend, as it were, by defiles cut through groves of fir and chestnuts, which make the traveller forget the asperity of the ascent.

Arriving at Gea, which stands about one, third of the way between the base and the summit of the mountain, the eye was gratified with a highly panoramic view of this wild and diversified country, and which may be called the Switzerland or the Highlands of Portugal; the latter indeed with the utmost propriety, as we found the hardy sons of the kilt, the brave 42nd regiment, quartered here. To one so long accustomed to scenes of desolation and misery, every thing seemed to put on a new and enchanting existence. The inhabitants appeared to live in comfort'—that expressive word which comprehends all which we usually understand by peace and plenty. I was delighted to renew my acquaintance with the feathered tribes of the barn-door; those *raræ aves* in the part of Portugal we had quitted. The town itself was just what it appeared in viewing it from a distance— the houses good, and the Praza excellent.

After completing some arrangements with General Clinton, we directed our steps towards the palace of Luis Bernardo, a great *fidalgo*, and brother to the Bishop of Guarda. Mr. —— had known him in the time of Sir John Moore; since which period he had not seen him. Our surprise was great and painful upon arriving at the spot, to find nothing but the ruins of this once magnificent edifice. We learnt, however, that the family still inhabited a small tenement adjoining the ruins, which in happier times had been the conservatory, and was now transformed into a comfortable sort of dwelling-house in the cottage style. Luis Bernardo came out immediately to welcome his old friend *Señor* Diego (by which name Mr. —— was known to him); and the profusion of embraces and kind words which the old man bestowed upon his unexpected guest, may be conceived, but cannot be described. He was quite enraptured; but in hinting at his misfortunes his countenance fell, and pointing to his ruined palace, which the French had destroyed, he became overwhelmed with a flood of tears.

In a few minutes his lady entered—a fat little person, dressed to the extreme of the fashion. She had been the mother of twenty-three children. Her joy at recognizing *Señor* Diego was not less unbounded than what her husband had just testified; and *"Maria Purissima!—Amigo mio!—Amiga mio antiguo!"* burst from her lips with unaffected volubility.

We dined by ourselves, as this was a fast-day with Bernardo and his family. The dinner was superb, and ample enough for a dozen visitors. We were served on massy plate, which the old gentleman said had only been disinterred from its hiding-place in the garden since the capture of Badajos. In the evening we were introduced to the three daughters of Señor Luis, and to the Padre of the family. The young ladies conversed in very good English, having been educated at Lisbon, where our language is looked upon as an essential branch of polite education.

I found the *Señor Padre* a very agreeable and well-informed companion, and he gave me a good deal of information respecting the chain of mountains known to the Romans by the name of Mons Herminius, of which the Estrella are a part. That point of the Sierra near Govea, which I have already noticed, is supposed to be the place from which Viriatus* rushed upon the Romans and drove

---

* This Viriatus is extolled by Cicero as one of those magnanimous freebooters who are remarkable for their equitable distribution of the plunder among their own confederates—a kind of Rinaldo Rinaldini.

them through Vizeu, the plains of which latter place are distinctly seen from Gea. There are three or four lakes on the top of these mountains; the Lagoa Rodonda, in ascending to Sabugiero, Lagoa Comprida, near Manteigas, and the Lagoa Escura, in that part of the chain known by the name of the Sierra de Cantaro, which rises above the other part of the ridge in the form of a pyramid; the lake being on its summit. The Padre assured me—I do not stipulate for your belief—that whenever there is a storm on the Portuguese coasts between Aveiro and the Mondego, the waters of this lake become very much troubled; and in a history of Spain and Portugal written by one Joao Vaseo, that author affirms that he himself saw some fragments of ships taken out of this lake.

These waters abound with a sort of fish, which I suppose, from the Padre's description, to be the char. The rivers Mondego and Zizery have their sources in these mountains—the last discharges itself into the Tagus at Punhetta with great fury and impetuosity, and its waters are distinguishable from those of its great recipient for a considerable length of course, by their gravely colour, while the stream of the Tagus itself is remarkably clear.

After breakfasting with Señor Luis, we set forwards on our journey, and dined with the commissariat officer stationed at Gallizes. I mention this, because during dinner a note was brought to him, which afterwards became the means of procuring us a night's lodging very opportunely. The billet was penned by the fair hand of Signora Maria Joze, niece to the *Capitaõ Maïor* of La Roza, distant three leagues from Gallizes. It appeared to have been written under much alarm, and for the purpose of receiving some advice as to the course she ought to pursue under the following circumstances:

A British major who had been quartered at the house,

purchased at his departure Maria Joze's palfrey; and after having had him in possession ten days, had sent him back under pretence of his not being suitable, and requesting to have the purchase-money returned. Signora Maria not having yielded to his demands, had that morning received a letter from him, threatening her with the resentment of the commandant at Celorico, who, he said, was about to send a detachment to make her prisoner. This was of course a mere fiction.

In the evening we mistook the road; and having wandered about an hour, without knowing whither, we found ourselves at length entering a village, which proved afterwards to be La Roza, and a good league from the road which we ought to have kept. The inhabitants had all retired to sleep; but arriving before a large and handsome house, we commenced such a battery at the door as soon brought someone to the window. All admittance was obstinately refused, on account of the lateness of the night. Enquiring where the *Juiz* lived, we were told that there was no *Juiz* in the place.

"Where do officers then apply for billets?" said we.

"Usually here, the residence of the Capitaõ Maïor," was the reply.

I suspected immediately whereabouts we were, and resolved to practise a military stratagem, in order to gain admittance.

"Pray", said I, "is not this La Roza?"

"Si, Signor," said the voice of some aged person.

"Is there not one Signora Maria Joze living here?"

"Si, Signora, si," eagerly replied some young woman concealed partly behind a balcony.

"Then," said I, pointing to Mr. ——, "here is the *commandant* of Celorico."

The doors were opened to us in a minute or two, our

horses led away to the stable, and we were cordially received by the *Capitaõ Maïor*. Maria Joze soon made her appearance, and we immediately recognized the voice which had addressed us from the window. With true feminine impatience she was for entering directly upon an explanation; but we observed rather dryly, that it would be better to defer it till after supper. The hint was not thrown away; and having ourselves repaired to the kitchen for the sake of the fire, we soon witnessed very substantial preparations going forward under the careful superintendance of Maria Joze.

After supper the cause was heard in great form by Mr. ——, and the pleasing judgment recorded "that Signora Maria Joze was not bound in justice to take back the horse." The best wine was now produced. Maria Joze, who was really handsome, though not very young, appeared quite fascinating, and the old *Capitaõ* became extremely facetious. On the following morning we were regaled with a sumptuous breakfast; the fragments of which were duly transferred by Maria in person to the capacious pockets of the *alforge** belonging to a sumpter-mule. The most unpleasant part now remained, that of undeceiving mine host and fair hostess; but so far were they from feeling offended, that they seemed to enjoy the joke mightily, and we parted the best friends in the world. We took care, however, to let them understand that the ungallant letter of the major had nothing in it at which they ought to be alarmed, for that the threat respecting the *commandant* of Celorico was pure fiction.

Mr. ——, in front of the Busaco Sierra, which we were now approaching, recapitulated the leading features of the memorable battle fought here in September 1810, when Massena was advancing upon Lisbon with his army of 90,000 men.

---

* An *alforge* is a capacious pair of saddle-bags.

The position of the British and Portuguese infantry was on the ridge of the Sierra, which is semicircular, and our line extended seven miles. We plainly discovered the Carmelite convent which formed the extreme left of our position, and also the spot where General Hill effected his well-timed junction. General Paine was stationed *at* the base of the ridge with his cavalry, while that of the enemy occupied the opposite villages. The Portuguese fought so well, that the French said they were Englishmen dressed in Portuguese uniforms. Massena beaten at every point where he attacked, manoeuvred extremely well. Not being able to force our position, he withdrew his troops silently round the north end of the Sierra, and gained the high road to Coimbra, which movement compelled Lord Wellington to fall back upon the lines. Massena thought us in full retreat, and that we should embark at Lisbon.

Full of this persuasion he pushed on, leaving his sick behind, and taking no measures whatever for the supply of his army. His surprise was of course any thing but an agreeable one, when he found our army safely entrenched behind those impregnable barriers which Lord Wellington had, with singular foresight, taken care to form as soon as he landed in the Peninsula. After his well known sojourn before our lines without being able to effect the least impression, Massena and his army became compelled by famine to retire upon Santarem, whither Lord Wellington pursued him.

We arrived in the afternoon at Raiva on the Mondego, after a march of six long leagues, not much short of thirty miles English. Raiva is a place of no note, nor will you be able to find it on your map, as it consists only of a few salt-houses. It is, however, a place of great importance to us at present, as the Mondego beyond this ceases to be navigable, and we have large magazines formed here, from which all the troops on the Estrella line draw their supplies. It is distant four leagues from Coimbra.

On the following day we set off for Fozdao in order to return towards Almeida by the Vizeu road. Our route lay along the banks of the Mondego for about a league, and we then ascended an exceedingly steep mountain, from the summit of which we descried the conflux of the Dao and the Mondego. On a little peninsula between the two is Fozdao, which we were desirous of reaching. When we surveyed it, however, from the dizzy height at which we had arrived, the steepness of the descent, and the extreme narrowness of the path on which we were standing—where if the horse had tripped or become alarmed, one plunge would have precipitated us into the gulf beneath—occasioned sensations of no pleasing nature. I felt an involuntary shuddering, and dismounted through cowardice. We were some minutes before we could discover any track by which we could descend, and at length after a most tortuous and fearful route we gained the river side, and were ferried over the Mondego to the little port of Fosdao.

A magazine was established here under charge of a Portuguese commissary. The other houses were all appropriated to the reception of salt, a commodity which confers on this small place some share of commercial importance. It is collected here in large quantities from Figuera, at the mouth of the Mondego, and circulated hence throughout the adjacent parts of Portugal, and even into Spain. We had quarters this night at Ova, a village on the Vizeu road, and in the house of a hospitable old prior.

On the following day we set out for Vizeu. At Santa Combadao, a short league from Ova, we paid our respects to the *Capitaõ Maïor*, who lives in a princely house, which Massena did him the favour to visit and plunder as he was advancing to the attack of Buzacos.

A journey of six long leagues brought us to Vizeu, a town which ranks next to Coimbra, and from which it is eighteen leagues distant. The streets are as good as any in Oporto, if you except the Rua Nova, and the shops are excellent. A bishop's palace, cathedral and prison are all adjoining each other.

Without the town are the remains of a Roman camp, and the ruins of some towers built by the same people, by whom this place was called Visoncium. What with the guards who are quartered here, and its being a general hospital station, Vizeu is at present quite thronged; we shall remain here a few days, and then return to Almeida on our way to Gallicia, on the frontiers of which it is possible we shall take up our winter-quarters.

Braganza, January 8, 1813

It is now nearly a week since we arrived in this city, where we are likely to remain until the army once more begin to move forward. On the 25th *ultimo* we left Almeida for the province of the Tras os Montes. We were attended by a Portuguese escort, as a security for 20,000*l.* in specie which we were carrying with us, to be appropriated to the purchase of cattle in Gallicia. The day of our departure was ushered in by a deep fall of snow, so much so, that our baggage mules were able to perform but a very short journey, and we were compelled to stay the first night at Figueira only four leagues from Almeida. As it was, it was nearly midnight before the baggage came in. We were fortunate in meeting with some pleasant society, who assembled to an evening *turtullia* given by the commissariat officer stationed here. A Spanish family from Madrid was of the party, and the evening passed very agreeably in music and dancing. After supper we were entertained with some patriotic songs, in which the Spanish ladies were the principal performers. The words of these are generally indifferent, often absurd, but are arranged to wild and plaintive national airs, which fall upon the ear with pleasing melody. The following is a stanza of one which I begged from the brother of one of the Madrid ladies, and I wish I could have procured the music, which was really very pretty. The words, you will see, are a curious mixture of the impassioned with the burlesque.

Al arma, al arma, Espagñoles;
La patria nos llama, corramos
Al arma, à vengarla fieles,
O' como buenos mueramos!
No á credulas esperanzas.
El pecho abrais; en tardando
Todo es perdido, y los grillos*—
Oh! baldon!** pude nombrarlos?

There is nothing in this that makes the faintest approach to the inspiring poetry of Tyrtasus, the war-songs of the German Gleim, or to any of the Scottish pieces; and some of the other stanzas are full of a very coarse low humour; and yet it is true that songs of this description often have a greater influence upon the people for whom they are written, than those wherein the poetry is of a higher order. It is Hume, if I recollect, who has not thought it beneath his historical dignity to remark that "Lillibullero" forwarded the revolution of 1688; and we know that in the first American war ridicule of this kind was a very successful engine in promoting the cause of Independence. The Spaniards, however, seem to have more taste for singing than fighting, while the poor Portuguese, who sing little and write no bad verses, fight like heroes.

As we advanced on our route we began to descry the distant summits of the Tras os Montes. The deep snow of the preceding day was rapidly dissolving, and the sun shone out with the warmth of an English May. At Castel Melhor we saw the remains of a Moorish castle, built on a steep hill, the inspection of which scarcely repaid the trouble of the ascent.

We were now approaching the pass of the Duero, or rather of the Coa, which discharges itself here into the

---

* The French are understood by *grillos*, "grasshoppers" or "locusts".
** *Oh! baldon!* "Oh! reproach!" This word was formerly written *baldron* and *baladron* from the Latin *balatro*.

Duero, a little below Quinta d'Orgal. After a descent of about one mile by a road extremely rugged and laborious, we gained the banks of the Coa, and crossed to the opposite shore. There is no ferry from the Quinta d'Orgal side over the Duero. The ascent from the Coa to the town of Villa Nova Fos Coa is not less than four miles. We halted here for the night, and the *Juiz de Fora* insisted upon receiving us into his own house, and on our departure gave us a letter of introduction to his brother *Señor* Moira, who holds the same official post at Braganza.

The whole of the next day was consumed over a march of little more than three leagues. The mules, which carried each 4000 dollars, could scarcely keep their feet in the precipitous track by which we once more descended upon the Duero. Arriving there at length, we found a bark sufficiently capacious to receive our whole cavalcade at once, amounting to twenty-one mules and horses. The current is here at all times very rapid; at the present time much more so than usual; and it was with considerable difficulty, and not without drifting far out of our course, that we succeeded in disembarking on the Tras os Montes shore. The remainder of the road to Torre de Moncorvo was excessively toilsome, though every pains had been bestowed upon the road in order to relieve the asperity of the ascent.

Moncorvo is an excellent town, with good streets, an extensive praça, and one of the most sumptuous churches which I have seen in Portugal. There is here too an unfinished castle magnificently built of white free-stone, within which the *Alcaldi** Maïor* has his residence. Also two prisons

---

* *Alcaldi, Alcaide.* This term for a magistrate is more peculiar to Spain than Portugal, and we met with it for the first time in Moncorvo. It is of course an Arabic word, as the article *Al* prefixed testifies. Formerly there were several classes of *alcaldis, viz. alcaldis* of the king's household, *alcaldis* of districts or chancelleries, *alcaldis de las aldeas,* or villages, &c. In Spanish romances any person with a venerable beard is complimented with the title of *alcaldi.*

and a convent for men. I was quartered in the house of a *fidalgo* who held the rank of Colonel of *Ordinanzas*. He had a large family of daughters, who were totally invisible, this being what they call a *casa grave*, "grave house ". The men servants were all excluded from the interior, and the entrance to the kitchen and women's apartments were as closely secured as any Turkish *harem*.

Leopold Henriques, the patron, was extremely liberal in his entertainment. He asked me a thousand questions during supper respecting female education in England, and whether there were not some Catholic convents, as he had an idea of sending his family over to be educated.

On the following morning we sent our baggage and escort forward by the direct road to Braganza, while we ourselves determined upon keeping the one beneath the crest of the Duero mountains, in order to have some conversation as to the resources of the Tras os Montes with the *Capitaõ Maïor* of Castello Branco. Previous to leaving Moncorvo, *Señor* Leopold, in answer to some enquiries, gave me a pleasing account of the fertility of this part of the country.

In the extensive vale of Villarica, which begins at about two leagues from Moncorvo on the direct road to Braganza, *canimo* or flax grows in great abundance and with surprising luxuriance, often reaching fifteen palms; *trigo* or wheat yields eighteen for one, and Indian corn 250 and 300 for one. Flax is ripe in August, *trigo* in June, and Indian corn in September. The fields are wonderfully productive of melons, and the olives are larger and redder than those produced in the Beira. Instead of the ordinary press for obtaining the oil, they here make use of a curious machine of straw plaited together, called *ceiria**, through which the oil filters.

---

* The word *ceiria* is derived, I think, from the Latin *seria*, which was an oblong vase in which oil, wine, and salt were preserved by the Romans; sometimes money as well.

Leaving Moncorvo for Castello Branco, our attention was soon drawn towards a mountain rising from the plain like a cone, and covered from base to summit with pines and firs. It had evidently, at some preceding period, been volcanic, as we picked up several pieces of lava on the road. It is known to the peasantry by the name of Cabesa dos Muiros (Moor's head). Having heard that there were the remains of some sepulchres visible near the summit, we pressed two peasants as our guides, and began to ascend, leaving our horses and servants in an adjoining field. Our guides thought us frantic, and crossed themselves for wonder when they heard we were ascending for the pleasure of looking for some tombs. We surprised a wild pig who was slumbering in the thicket, and regretted not having provided ourselves with a fowling-piece. When we reached the summit, there was an appearance of what might have been a crater, but neither sepulchres nor relics of any description.

We had consumed so much time in this undertaking, that it was dark when we reached Quinta das Cobradas, and we had half a league more to Castello Branco. The *regidor* of the village, upon discovering that we were Englishmen and on our way to the *Capitaõ Maïor*, offered to become our guide. His services were very acceptable, as from the intricacy of the road, and the darkness of the night, we should in all probability have lost our way. The *Capitaõ Maïor* was on the point of retiring to rest when we arrived. His house was truly magnificent, nor did he disparage it by any lack of hospitality.

On the following day our route lay through Mogaduro, a place of very considerable antiquity. We found the *Juiz de Fora* living within a castle, originally Moorish, part of which, in the interior space, had been converted into a convenient dwelling-house.

At Algoso we crossed the Sobor by a beautiful bridge of Moorish architecture, and on the heights above were the ruins of a castle, built by the same warlike people, for the purpose of commanding the passage of the river. We passed the night at Outeiro, and having on the following morning paid our respects to the *Capitaõ Maïor*, who inhabits a good house on the *raia* or frontier, we set forwards for Braganza, distant from Outeiro three leagues. We were delighted with the idea of having reached our winter-quarters, and called immediately upon *Señor* Moira, the *Juiz de Fora*, and presented his brother's letter. The bishop's palace was assigned to Mr. —— for a billet, and I received one for myself upon Señor Garcia, a wealthy woollen-draper, with an intimation that any other in the town should be at my command, with the exception of those houses inhabited by the clergy, who are very numerous in Braganza, and all exempted from military requisition.

Here then, in the titular city of the crown of Portugal, we are destined to pass the winter; and happy, thrice happy may we deem ourselves in being removed for a season from those scenes of fearful misery and desolation, which shock the sight in but too many other parts of this fruitful kingdom.

Braganza has never known the horrors of war. The French, indeed, in the time of Sir John Moore, attempted its capture, but were repulsed by the brave peasantry who inhabit the *raia*. This city retains therefore all its original pride; and her second boast is, that her merchants are as honourable as they are wealthy. Here, it is said, a bankruptcy has never been known. On approaching the city from the Miranda side, there is nothing of it discoverable but the castle, until you are on the point of entering. The castle itself is now in a state of ruin, although part of the walls are yet in good preservation, and furnished with some rusty cannon.

Within its precincts are a number of little tenements, which serve as barracks to the militia of the place. Descending from the castle hill, you look down upon the town, which, in its leading features, consists of two principal streets, running parallel to each other for about half-a-mile, terminating in an extensive *praça*, and thence diverging under new names to the right and left.

The palace of the bishop is a magnificent building. His lordship however resides at Castro, a little village about one league distant, and in a very humble mansion. The palace is under the care of one of his private chaplains. The clergy here are rich, and, as far as I can see, very much respected. There is a peculiarity in the costume of the canons which I have nowhere else observed—except among the partridges—which is, that they are all red-legged, their stockings being of a bright crimson. There are two convents for women in the city; one appropriated solely to the reception of females of noble rank, the other much inferior both in point of wealth and discipline. To this last I have paid several visits, and they make no scruple to open the upper half of the door in the vestibule, where we are allowed to converse with the nuns under the surveillance of two or three of the more ancient damsels of the order.

Braganza, January 21, 1813

In my future letters I will endeavour to send you, since you desire it, as correct an itinerary as I can. On the main roads the distance is always to be found pretty correctly stated in a published *routeiro* of the country; but whenever we move out of this track we are then left to our own calculation of distance, or to the uncertain information of the peasantry. To shew you how little dependence is to be placed upon this last method, I will relate what took place a few days ago.

I was anxious to reach a village on the frontiers of Gallicia by an early hour in the morning; accordingly I left Braganza at daybreak, having been previously told that the distance was four leagues, and that such a village was midway. I rode forwards, passed the half-way-house, and beginning to think myself near the end of the journey, I inquired of a peasant:

"How far to Monzalves?"

"A league and a half," was the reply.

In less than five minutes after this, I put the same question to a countryman coming along on mule-back:

"*Huma legoa chiquita*" (a very short league) said he, casting down his eyes rather proudly on his ambling beast.

Almost immediately afterwards an old goatherd affirmed Monzalves to be distant "a good league "(*huma legoa boa*).

The fact is, the one took his ideas of distance from the

speed of his mule; the other from his usual rate of walking, which, from his age, would be none of the fastest. My next informant told me that Monzalves was *"muito perto"* (very near). Another, after I had ridden a long mile, described it as being at the distance of *"huma tirar de balo"* (within musket-shot). At length, after riding at least half a mile further, I discovered the village in a valley beneath me, and then had a hill in front, which took a good quarter of an hour to descend.

I shall now give you some account of our first expedition into Spain. This city, as I told you I believe in my last, is to be our head-quarters for the winter, and from which, as from a centre, we shall make excursions into the neighbouring provinces, for the purpose of ascertaining the resources of the country against another campaign, and of drawing from it such supplies of cattle as they may afford.

The 14th and 15th of this month being fair-days at Outeiro and Miranda de Duero, we set off for the former on the evening of the 13th. I was quartered in the house of one Francisco Martel, the venerable father of a numerous progeny. His sons, seven in number, were all soldiers; and he related it as a singular boast, that not one had ever deserted.

On the following day, a good many head of cattle were brought in for sale; but a report having been circulated that we intended to embargo them, and to settle with the owners by bills on the military chest at head-quarters, they all disappeared in less than an hour. It was in vain we announced, through the medium of the *escrivano*, that all purchases should be paid for at Braganza; our credit was not yet established. There was a brisk sale for iron, which was brought in considerable quantity from Gallicia. Among the Spaniards present at the fair were a few officers of the army attached to the Intendancy of Valladolid, now sitting at a frontier town called Trabessas. We found the same distrust of us at Miranda which we had experienced at Outeiro. Not a single bullock was to be seen. I was quartered in the house of a bragging, talkative fellow named Joaõ Baptisto, who had published an account of his own patriotism, and which he said he should be proud to lay at "my lordship's feet".

This city is now rapidly verging to decay, owing to the stagnation of trade, which is all transferred to Braganza, The cathedral is a sumptuous pile, built of remarkably fine freestone. On approaching the altar, my attention was drawn towards a curious little figure, about six inches high, dressed in a short jacket, and holding a small globe of crystal in his hand. My conductor could only inform me that he was a "saint"; and confirmed his assertion by crossing himself most devoutly.— The Praça is tolerable; and at the farther end of the town, towards Spain, are the remains of a fine Moorish castle, with its battlements and turrets in excellent preservation.

We went down to inspect the Duero; for, in the event of the army advancing, Miranda might become an advantageous spot for a large depot, since supplies could be thrown direct from it upon Salamanca, from which it is distant only fourteen leagues. The scenery of the Duero is awfully wild and grand. From a dizzy height you look down upon it, foaming along its craggy bed, while the ascent on the other side appears impracticable, and presents to the eye nothing but a wall of nearly perpendicular rocks, of which the eagles and other birds of prey seem to have undisturbed possession. The descent from the Portuguese side is nearly two-thirds of a mile; and the passage across the river is effected by three ropes which play upon each other through running blocks secured to a scaffolding, and worked by a wheel.

On account of the fair there was a good deal of passage from the Spanish side. The men twist their heels over the

71

rope, having their waists secured to it by a cord, and holding on by their hands. The women contrive to sit in a sling, and in this way are drawn across with surprising expedition. It was amusing to see a party consisting of half a dozen men and women, two or three cows, and some noisy pigs, all brought over at the same time. In summer the current is less rapid, and cattle could easily be swum across.

We visited a convent of the order of the cross. At present it contains only six monastics. There are but two of this order in Portugal, the second being at Mirandella, where the Superior resides. We called upon the widow of the late Intendant of Zamora, who was murdered by the peasantry three years ago on account of his supposed attachment to the French. This may serve to illustrate the difference between the two countries—the nobles in Portugal rule the peasants, the peasants in Spain rule the nobles. The widow, with her four nieces, one of them a beautiful girl of sixteen, lives in a state of sorry exile; the greatest part of their property having been plundered during the massacre of her husband.

Previous to quitting this city for Spain, the staff of the Miranda regiment paid us a visit, accompanied by a Spaniard whose name and title, as per card, ran thus— *"Don Melchor, Reggio Commissionado e Cavalh'ero do distinguido ordem de Carlos III."* He gave us a letter to his friend General Renovales who was residing at Carvijalas. He described the cattle resources of Spain as next to infinite, and assured us that the pound of meat would not cost more than two *reals* (one-tenth of a dollar). He also gave us to understand that the person who could furnish the best information on the subject was Don Andres O'Rian of Tabara, an Irishman by birth, and employed by Lord Wellington on *observation,* which is an honourable expression for a spy. The *Commissionado* was a fine manly fellow, a complete contrast to my vulgar and self-satisfied patron Joaõ Baptisto.

We slept this night, the 16th, at Paradella, a frontier village, and the following morning set forwards on our journey. A little river divides Portugal in this part from Spain, and which we no sooner crossed than, as if by magic, pigs with their provender, the bellota*, and corn-fields met the eye.

We soon came to Castro. It being Sunday the villagers were at mass. A smart lively woman was on the point of tripping into church when we arrived. Upon telling her we wished to hear mass, *"Vamos! Senhores,"* cried she, and waited as though to chaperone us. The difference between the Spanish and Portuguese women could never be better seen than in the instance before us. This lively Spaniard was certainly approaching what is called the regulation age; but yet her open manners, her graceful gait, and the youthfulness of the Spanish costume gave her the attractive air of a girl. When it was whispered within the sacred precincts that Englishmen were in the village, the curate and *alcaldi* came out to welcome us. Religion was suspended, and the *Señor* Padre was so complaisant as to say, that if we would only wait until he had finished mass, which he assured us he would do with all possible expedition, we should be welcome to his house and chocolate. The country here is open and fertile, and seemed to abound in mineral springs. A good many Merino rams and cattle were pasturing in the meadows.

At about a league in advance from Castro we descended into a most charming valley. The reflection of the winter's sun was so strong that it was as warm as an English May, although the tops of the mountains were covered with snow. Through this valley runs the little river Liska, and surely if ever stream was worthy of the muse's praise, Liska is enti-

---

* The bellota is the acorn of the evergreen oak which is one of the distinguishing features of Spanish scenery.

tled to her share. A rustic bridge for foot-passengers was thrown across it, and innumerable flocks of sheep and goats were browsing its luxuriant pastures. The stream abounds in trout, perch, and a fish they call *boga*, which I suppose to be the dace. Upon ascending the opposite hill we saw Muga on the left, and near it the ruins of a castle. In advancing from this upon our place of destination, we were thrown into a little alarm. We were now within three leagues of the French, or perhaps nearer, as their outposts extended close to the banks of the Ezla. As we were talking of this, three cavalry, apparently in French costume, began to descend a hill in front of us. Upon observing us they stopped, and one of them went back as if for the purpose of protecting a woman who was following at some little distance. A droll kind of pause now ensued.

Mr. —— and myself were well armed, and our two Portuguese servants indifferently so. Putting ourselves therefore into the most martial order we could, we galloped up to them and demanded who they were. They drew out their passports, and proved themselves to be our friends the guerrillas.

We learnt from them that the French have a force of about 1000 men only in Zamora, and that an equal number with a detachment of *gens-d'armes* had, a few days before, taken possession of Benavente. They conceived we should be in no danger of a surprise at Carvijalas, as the Ezla was considerably swollen, and the Spaniards had secured the boats to their own side. Near Benavente, however, is the bridge called Puente de St. Crastino, but then there are detachments of guerrillas in all the villages on our side the river, *viz.* at Mansinal, St. Vincente, St. Pedrico, and Perilla de Castro. About three o'clock in the afternoon we entered Carvijalas, and procured a billet from the *Escrivano*.

As soon as we were established in our quarters, we paid a visit to General Renovates. Mr. —— kept back the introductory letter, until he saw what reception he would give us as Englishmen. He was freezingly polite, and felt ashamed to be thawed into cordiality when we presented him with the epistle from his "*buen amigo*, Don Melchor." From his house we proceeded to that of the ex-governor of Zamora, who received us with every kindness and hospitality. Dinner was on the point of being served up, and he insisted upon our staying. Hungry travellers need little pressing. In the evening we had a pleasant *tertullia*, at which a number of Spanish ladies were present. We were here introduced to one Don Gabriel Maroto, who was stationed here on *observation*. Lord W. has nearly twenty persons similarly employed on this side of the Ezla, who transmit accounts to head-quarters of whatever falls under their notice.

On the following morning I strolled about to take a view of the town, which can boast of not more than half-a-dozen city-like houses, the rest having the long-running low roofs which characterize the village. The church has nothing remarkable about it. The walls are covered with miserable daubs of paintings, all of which relate, as usual, to miracles.

The following is an inscription written beneath one of these hallowed tablets, whereon is depicted a man lying on a sick bed, and praying devoutly to the Virgin Mary, who is represented as peeping at him from behind a curtain—

Bernardo Casado San Juan Vicino y Ess^{no} desta Villa, estando infiermo de Accidientes e desauciado offricieron a S^{ma} de 1' Carmen i luego sano. a.d. 1702.

There was another picture of the 11,000 virgins, but upon what occasion, or where so many were assembled together, I must leave to your researches to discover*. They were probably not of Spanish origin. Opposite to this there was a large picture of St. Nicholas raising up souls from purgatory. Behind the church is a grammar-school, where I found the senior boys reading Phaedrus! We left Carvijalas at noon on our return to Braganza. At Muga, which I have before noticed, we had some conversation with the *alcaldi*, with the view of getting him to use his influence with the peasantry to send in their cattle for sale to Braganza. We told him that it was during the winter season that we must provide resources for striking another blow against *"los picoros Franceses"*, but all our efforts to kindle in him the flame of patriotism were answered with a frigid *"bien"*.

Alcanizes, distant four leagues from Carvijalas, is a tolerably good town. Here we found the Intendancy of Valladolid, which had removed from Trabessas to this place two days before our arrival. The Intendant was abundantly civil, and in pleading his inability to forward our views, regretted his not having any authority in this district; but the truth is, he *could* do a great deal, but will not.

We stayed the night at Trabessas, and had quarters in the house of the curate. He, good easy man, was too agreeably occupied with the conversation of his niece, who had just returned from a distant visit, to spare us much of his company. It is a little singular that almost five *cures* out of ten whom I have met with, have always an inmate possessing no ordinary pretensions to beauty; and this singularity is furthermore increased by the pretty inmate being invariably the good man's niece.

We reached Braganza next morning in time for the fair, but although there were nearly 2500 head of cattle for sale,

---

* According to the legend, St. Ursula and 11,000 virgins were sent into Britain to be married to Conon and his knights, about the end of the 4th century, and were either martyred on the sea by the barbarous people, or by Attila, king of the Huns.

we could only succeed in purchasing 120, and those at the average of as many dollars each, i. e. about 36*l.* per head, at the present rate of exchange. Is not this a frightful price? especially when you consider that they will not average more than 300lb by the time they reach the army, and they must even travel well to do that. As the 5th division on the Duero are entirely dependent upon us for their supply, we are obliged to purchase; but I hope that our unwillingness to give the extravagant prices asked by the dealers will have the effect of lowering the market.

A few days ago I was at Vinhaes, a very pleasant town four leagues from this on the road to Mirandella. I could only purchase forty-two head, and at exorbitant prices. I saw a pair of draught oxen, the property of General Barcellas, sold for fifty *moidores*, equivalent, at the present exchange, to 90*l*! I was billetted on a *fidalgo*, who entertained me sumptuously, and we had large dinner and evening parties both the days which I remained with him. There are many magnificent houses in this town belonging to the nobility, the greater part of whom, however, had gone to Lisbon for the winter.

Braganza, February 20, 1813

I am miserably disappointed in Braganza; it is the dullest place I ever saw, and I now begin to regret even my poor quarters in Almeida, which stood so hospitably open to the wind and rain. There, I had always the governor's house to resort to, when in want of society, and it was seldom that a day passed without having myself an opportunity of being hospitable to some British officer passing through. General —— now and then leaves his command at ——, and comes to us for a few days, for the purpose of gathering intelligence as to the movements of the French on the other side of the Ezla, but I suspect his reconnaissances tend also towards a different quarter.

The old governor, a florid, good-natured, white-headed gentleman of sixty, who always goes forth to the public in a most exaggerated gold-laced cocked hat, is married to a very pretty woman, possessed of more grace and *naiveté* than what Nature lavishes upon Portuguese ladies in general. Her sister, Donna Mariana, lives with her; and the foul-mouthed chronicler says that the gallant general's attentions are well received by both ladies—the governor himself, good easy man, being *"Doctus spectare lacunar."*

So much for scandal, which in England is supposed to be the prerogative of tea-tables, where ladies sit in solemn inquest upon the deceased reputations of their neighbours. From what quarter do you suppose I foraged this dainty *morceau*? Do not suspect the women; they, poor things, are too well immured from all the rumours of this naughty world! Not to trifle with your time, my informant was *Padre* Martinho, one of the chaplains of the bishop, who takes care of the palace.

The Bishop, Don Antonio de Veiga, descended from one of the first families in Portugal, and not an alien from royal blood, lives almost in monastic retirement at the little village of Castro, about one mile from the city. Some years ago he was, I understand, arraigned at Lisbon upon charges of no less a nature than incontinency and sorcery. Some circumstances of a very revolting nature transpired upon this occasion. The enquiry took place in consequence of a nun (whose situation would not allow of concealment) having blasphemously given out that she had been favoured in a similar manner as the Virgin Mother was in the days of Herod. She had even presented the bishop with some phials of her milk, and by which his Excellency was said to have wrought the cure of various diseases. People came to him from remote parts of both countries to be healed of their infirmities: and it was but the other day that I met a peasant, subject to epilepsy, on his road to Castro for the same purpose. The nun, I believe, had the miserable fate of being strangled at Lisbon shortly after the trial.

Mr. —— and myself paid our respects to him a few days ago, and he received us with such an air of humility! His hands crossed upon his breast; his eyes bent downwards on the ground; while a faint smile of inexpressible *significancy* played upon his pallid but highly expressive countenance. He is deeply read in ancient and modern history; and I felt truly ashamed when he touched upon some points in our own annals, in which I stood convicted of gross ignorance. With respect to religious liberty, he made no scruple to let us see the liberality of his opinions; and I believe it would be no difficult matter to bring him to avow that the Pope is the chief heretic.

He said, "that the mental errors of men, while the great truths of religion are maintained, are but as dust in the balance, and do not merit those damnatory prohibitions and rancorous persecutions with which they have been so often punished." Could this be said, do you think, in sincerity? He certainly spoke with much warmth; whether real or affected I do not know: but how can he, if such be his genuine sentiments, carry on these pious frauds? (not to call them by a worse name).

A few days after this conversation, Mr. —— received a long letter from him on the subject of civil and religious liberty. On the last he said, he hoped that the English, who enjoyed the peculiar and inestimable privilege of *"Habeas Corpus"*, were equally blessed with that of the *"Habeas Animum"*. Mr. —— has since forwarded the letter to His Royal Highness the Duke of Kent, as a literary curiosity of the country. The dissembling Tiberius, you know, in the commencement of his reign was wont to say, "the tongues of men in a free state ought also to be free."

Besides a bishop residing out of the town, we have an archbishop residing in the town, the Archbishop of Burgos, a venerable kind-hearted man, eighty years of age, who has come to Portugal in search of that peace and retirement which his own country at present does not afford. His income is small, and derived, I understand, from the voluntary contributions of the canons of Burgos, by whom he is greatly beloved. It is sufficient, however, for the support of a moderate establishment, although nothing in comparison with the princely revenue he formerly enjoyed. He has with him a private chaplain, an *amanuensis*, four servants, and a kind of state-carriage drawn by six mules. Nothing can exceed his detestation of the French, and particularly of Napoleon, of whom there is no story, how absurd soever it may be, but he religiously believes. His antipathy to *"los picoros"* is not to be wondered at, for he was soundly cudgelled, poor man, by the French soldiers during the treacherous business at Bayonne, and narrowly escaped with his life. I frequently make him a morning visit, and generally find his *amanuensis* reading to him, while he himself is employed in manufacturing his own soup! This is the simplest sort of pottage imaginable—some heads of garlic are kept simmering on the ashes in an earthen vessel which holds about two quarts of water; a few minutes before it is required for use, his Excellency puts in with his own episcopal hands, a certain quantity of red pepper and a small cup of oil; and the process is completed by pouring the whole over some thin slices of Spanish bread. I do not pretend to account for the apparent whimsicality of this conduct; it may arise, perhaps, from the doting humours of advanced age, from the weariness and inanity inseparable from a state of exile, or from a primitive simplicity of manners*.

The *amanuensis* as I entered the other morning was entertaining the venerable pre late with the account of a ludicrous pedigree of Napoleon and Josephine, and of the origin of the name "Buonaparte". His Excellency will not allow it to be a *pasquinade*, but holds it a piece of genuine history. In the same work, Murat, the Duke of Cleves, is made out to have been a tinker at Cahors, and after passing some gloomy years in kettle-mending, *"el tal Murat paso años atros remendado peroles",* was promoted to the post of waiter in the coffee-house of St. Sebastian at Madrid.

---

* A French author of the last century, who has been accused of wantonly decrying the customs and manners of the Spaniards, had probably met with a similar instance when he says— *"Les grands d'Espagne se font un friand ragoût d'un ail ou d'un oignon; qu'ils cadenacent une chaîne d'argent à leur pot, de peur que leurs domestiques ne mangent la viande qui est dedans."*

The only excursion which I have made since my last has been to head-quarters at Villa Formosa, a few leagues beyond Almeida.

The route from Braganza to Torre de Moncorvo I copy from my journal—

	Leagues	
From Braganza to Sortes	2	
Val Bemfeito	5	Small village, rich in corn.
Bornes	1	Large and flourishing town
St. Comba	2	Pretty village which you reach by a bad and craggy road
Junqueira	2	
Postella	1	
Moncorvo	1	

In approaching Junqueira, you descend upon the valley of Villarica, the fertility of which I have already mentioned. This rich vale is hemmed in by barren and lofty mountains. The little river of Villarica winds through it, and which you cross no less than seven times in the course of half a league.

From a first view of the province of the Tras os Montes, the traveller is not induced to think very favourably of its fertility and population, but upon closer inspection his opinion changes. Cultivation of no common order will often surprise him in the very bosom of sterility, and a cheerful village meet the eye where he least expected to find one.

I slept the second night at Postella, a place consisting of only two houses, both inns or *estalages*, one of them called Silvera, the other Postella. Here you cross the Sobor by a very pretty bridge of seven arches. The river at this spot sometimes rises fifty feet above its ordinary level, and the people of the *estalage* shew a mark half way up the side of their house, which is built on an eminence, where the water reached three years ago; but this only happens when the fresh of the Duero breaks in upon the current of the Sobor, which discharges itself into the former about half a league below the bridge, and, as it were, under Moncorvo.

I arrived at Almeida the following day, and took up my quarters in the hospitable mansion of the governor. I learnt from him, that he had it in contemplation to solicit a brigadiership in the Spanish service; and certainly, to a man of enterprising character, this service presents a wide field; one, so choked with weeds, that the flowers are scarce distinguishable. Their army is at present an incongruous and tumultuous mass. The delicate line which ought to run between the private and the officer is trampled on and effaced. A desire for military appearance, that sort of neatness bordering upon pomp, but never reaching it, is totally unknown. Soldiers and officers are alike slovens in their persons; or, if they do perchance make a display more than ordinary, it is but of a tawdry kind, like embroidery upon sackcloth. It is no small point gained to make a soldier proud of himself, i.e. of his dress, &c. And it is a curious fact, that black balls and pipe-clay have contributed more to the invincibility of our troops than you would imagine.

I spent a pleasant day or two with Captain ——, whose brigade is quartered at Gallegos, a few leagues on the Portuguese side of Ciudad Rodorigo. A large barn in this village has been converted into a temporary theatre, and the *company* has had the honour, during the winter, of exhibiting a number of pieces to "overflowing and brilliant houses." Captain —— is their chief man, stage-manager, and actor of first parts. A few weeks ago he appeared in "Zanga." Lord Wellington and his staff were present. On the next day his lordship took the field with his—fox hounds, and in the ardour of the chase, Captain —— was thrown from his horse into a river. Lord Wellington witnessed the catastrophe, and asked who it was. "It's only Zanga washing his face, my lord", said Colonel —— who was riding by. So much for head-quarter-hunting anecdote.

We now and then have a kind of hunting party of our own at Braganza, for which we are indebted to the miscellaneous pack of a sporting butcher in this city, by name Mendoza. He claims consanguinity with the little pugilistic hero of our own country, whose fame he has heard of, and supports his pretensions to the breed by having, on several occasions, shewn himself.

I have been amused this morning at seeing a number of jack-asses pass through from Gallicia. They were all of uncommon size and substance, and kept for the purpose of begetting mules. Their housings were sumptuous; and it was pleasant to see these poor creatures, so despised in many countries, led along by their owners with as much pride and care as if they had been stallions of Araby. The value of one of these animals varies from 60 to 100 guineas!

I must not omit to inform you of a discovery which I have made, *viz.* that Braganza is the Paradise of the Jews. The merchants and respectable shop-keepers are nearly all of this persuasion. It is true, they have no synagogue, and an open profession of their faith would endanger their lives—certainly their liberties. I understand, however, they meet privately among themselves, and celebrate the rites of their church as a sort of freemasonry, while in their outward behaviour, and their attendance at mass, they are hyper-catholics. The women have no communion whatever in the Levitical ceremonies.

22nd. The French have been ravaging Alcanizas, only four leagues from this, and are at this time near Puebla de Zenabria. The Archbishop of Burgos, and a number of the wealthier inhabitants, have precipitately left the place. General —— is here, and we ride out daily towards the frontiers in order to gain intelligence. His remark to me respecting the Spanish army is exactly similar to the opinion of the governor of Almeida— "The peasantry make the best soldiers in the world, but are headed by the worst of officers."

March 17, 1813

On the 1st instant we left Braganza on a tour into Gallicia. Our route was as follows:

	League
Orellos	1
Dine	2
Moimento	1
Monzalves	1½
Musquita	1

These are the distances as stated by the peasantry, for
here we have no *routeiro* to refer to.

At Moimento we crossed the little river of Tuela, and
entered upon Spain. Here we met with one of our cattle
dealers, driving on about 200 head of small cattle towards
Braganza, which he had purchased in the neighbourhood
of Lugo. We were detained so long in reviewing the herd,
and talking over the price to be paid, that it was nearly dark
when we resumed our journey.

We had not proceeded far before we began to apprehend
that we had mistaken the way. The traveller who thinks
of journeying here by roads and directions of places, will
frequently find himself egregiously mistaken. Portugal and
Spain, in some parts, are only to be known by trees, rocks,
mountains, or other features of nature, which remark holds
good of all wild and mountainous countries. Mr. ———, who
had been here before, luckily rescued us from a wide aber-
ration, by recognizing, at a little distance, a peculiar group

of trees on the other side of a ravine, and by which object we regained the right track for Musquita.

Quarters were assigned us by the *Alcaldi* in the house of the *Señor* Abbãt. This being the night of the *Entrudo*, called by us the eve of Shrove Tuesday, the village was one scene of music, merriment, and feasting: they seemed anxious to devour meat enough to support them during the approaching Lent. A large party was assembled at the abbot's. Masters and servants mingled in the same dance. It was a night of perfect equality, and passed away amidst "Quips and cranks and wanton wiles," such as lighting pieces of tow, and throwing them at each other's faces, sprinkling one another with flour, and filling their neighbour's shoes with cold water.

On the following day we continued our route, with the intention of reaching Las Hermitas before night, distant seven leagues. The route was as follows:

	League	
Pereiro	½	
Alcanizo	½	
Peishero	1	intermediate vil-
Viana	3	lages, Solvero, Suano,
		Montejo, Pinsa
Fornellos	½	
Chaô de Castro	½	
Las Hermitas	1	

Alcanizo is a small town, and very dirty, but at this point the amazing fertility of Gallicia began to open upon us. The prospect was extremely fine. In front of us rose a *sierra**, the crests of which were buried in the clouds, and capped with snow. In these mountains are stags, bears, and wolves. As we advanced, this *sierra* seemed to close round us like a vast amphitheatre, of which the interior space was diversi-

---

* The term *sierra*, peculiar to Spain and Portugal, denotes a chain of mountains, the successive peaks of which present the resemblance of a saw.

fied by hills, valleys, plains, and villages; the latter met the eye in every direction, and you no sooner entered any than you appeared always in the centre of a circle of them. The whole Gallician army, which is computed at 30,000, might be quartered here within a circumference of ten miles.

Upon descending from Pinsa upon Viana, we crossed the Bebay by a tolerable stone bridge. This river rises in a gap of the mountains in the direction of Puebla de Zenabria. Viana we found a dull looking town.

The Governor of Benavente had left it the day preceding our arrival. He had been over to inspect some cavalry which were here refitting; i. e. taking from the peasantry every horse they can find, without giving them any thing in return. These *Cavallieros* had suffered the French to cross the Esla a few weeks ago, and surprise their steeds, while they were engaged at a ball given by the governor in Benavente.

Arriving at Chaô de Castro, we inquired our way to Las Hermitas which lies out of the Lugo road. We were told that it was distant one league, and that upon arriving at a group of chestnut trees, we were to strike off to the left. In this country there is scarcely any twilight: almost immediately after sunset night comes on. This was our situation. At sunset we began to descend a mountain; and by a fatality not unusual with travellers in this country, found ourselves in a deep ravine, with a river before us, and no traces of any road. Shepherds' fires were gleaming in the distance, but the river was between us and them. We had no alternative but to re-ascend, and endeavour to fall in with some road which might conduct to a village. When we regained the heights, village lights appeared on every side; but by some "cantrip slight", as we advanced they seemed to recede.

At length, having crawled and stumbled about for upwards of two hours, as romances begin, (although it led to the end of our wanderings,) we heard a deep-toned bell; followed in the direction of the sound, and soon discovered a broad pathway. We had not descended (for we were again descending some mountain) more than a quarter of a mile, when we came to a little oratory, or temple.

"Here we are ", cried I.

About 200 yards farther, we came to a second, then to a third—fourth—in short, for a good mile there were nothing but temples.

"What are all these temples?" cried we to some persons standing before a group of houses, at which we had now arrived.

"They are the temples of Las Hermitas", replied a decrepit old man who was crawling up the road we had descended, with a lighted piece of charcoal between two sticks, and which he was continually blowing with his breath, to enable him to see his way.

"The Temples of Las Hermitas!" said we, "and where are you going at this time of night?"

"To say my prayers at the farthest temple", replied he; "my sins are many, and my penitence must be great—God be with you!"

We bid the old penitent goodnight, and addressed ourselves to some peasants who came out as it were to see who had arrived.

"Is this the village of Las Hermitas?"

"No! this is Loco, Hermitas is lower down."

We took one of these fellows for a guide, and after passing another little regiment of temples, arrived at our headquarters. We were not long in finding out the house of Francisco Junqueira, a great cattle dealer, where we solaced ourselves with a *potchero* of fowl, garlic, ham and cabbage, all stewed together.

On the following morning I arose with an impatience

to view the place at which it had cost us so much trouble to arrive. Beneath the windows of my bedroom dashed along the Bebay, a wild romantic stream, in one part clear and smooth as polished crystal; in another, broken by rocks, foaming and tumbling in waterfalls. An excellent stone bridge carries the traveller into the Orenze road; and in spite of the steepness of the mountains, which rise from the very brink of the river, the industrious Gallician has forced the culture of the vine nearly to their summit.

Returning from the bridge, my surprise was great at beholding, in so poor a village, the turrets of a magnificent cathedral, built about 400 years ago, as I afterwards learned, by two bishops of Astorga, and maintaining at present an *administrador* and four chaplains. To this cathedral and to these hermitages people come from all parts of the Peninsula. It is to many, as the temple at Mecca to the *Mahometans*—the maimed, the lame, the blind, penitents, and those devoted to religion from their youth, flock hither to offer up their prayers to the Virgin. The approach to this venerable pile is through a spacious court rather fancifully paved with various coloured pebbles. On the right hand side of this court, beneath an arcade, are twelve wooden figures, large as life, representing the Apostles. Judas Iscariot with a bottle (bag?) in his hand, and grinning most horridly, is accommodated with a corner to himself. The Apostles are all labelled, like so many vials in an apothecary's shop. At the farther end of this arcade is a figure of our Saviour being tied to a stake by the executioner of Pilate; and the artist, in order to excite, in a greater degree, an abhorrence for this unjust minister of justice, has embossed his face with a prodiguously large and disgusting nose.

While Mr. ——and myself were engaged in reviewing these figures, the loud swell of the organ burst upon our ears. We passed the palisades, which are surmounted

90

by lions rampant, and entered the church. It was the celebration of grand mass. The curtain before the Virgin was drawn up. The *administrador*, in gorgeous robes, was dropping his curtseys before the altar, which was illuminated with a profusion of wax tapers. Frankincense was being scattered about from silver censers, and I was in the act of persuading myself that the whole scene was very solemn and imposing, when I happened to turn my eye upon a pretty penitent, who commenced such a battery of glances as speedily to counteract any incipient feeling towards this splendid form of devotion.

After breakfast we paid a visit to the *administrador*.

Upon entering the hall, our attention was drawn towards an old-fashioned kind of arm-chair suspended from the end of a pair of steelyards; and we were soon given to understand that the offerings to the Virgin were regulated by the weight of the penitents. A lively girl informed us that her penitence had cost her 4½ *arrobas* of wheat; that is, she weighed about 144lbs. *avoirdupoise*.

The *administrador* was a good sort of old bigot, and, while we were sipping his chocolate, entertained us with a rich variety of miracles which had been performed by our "Lady of the Hermitages", and with an account of the number of distinguished persons who had visited and enriched her shrine, and of the extraordinary cures which had been vouchsafed to her suppliants. The conversation turning upon politics, he betrayed the greatest anxiety to learn whether it were undoubtedly true that Lord Wellington had been declared *Generalissimo* of Spain. The news had but just travelled into Gallicia; and from what he said, the greater part of the Spanish army were much discontented at his elevation to this rank.

Our conference with Francisco, the cattle-dealer, was so satisfactory, that we did not proceed on to Lugo as we had intended when we set out, but returned to Braganza by the same road we came, highly delighted with what we had seen of the fertility and beauty of this province.

The Gallicians are a plodding painstaking people. Strabo said of them in his time, that they were warlike, and difficult to subjugate. This, I apprehend, is not their character at present. They seem all to be *"paisibles casaniers "*, and are not *"fougeux"*, like the peasantry of Castille.

The population of Gallicia is computed at 1,200,000; but the number is small when compared with the extent and fertility of this part of the kingdom. In the time of Julius Caesar, the whole population of Spain was reckoned to be nearly 40,000,000; which, considering the immense armies they sent into the field, is perhaps not far from the truth. The language of Gallicia is a mixture of Portuguese with Spanish; which may be accounted for by the emigration of such great numbers of its inhabitants into Portugal; when after passing the greater part of their lives as *gallegos* in Lisbon or Oporto, they return to their own country, bringing back together with the earnings of their labour the dialect of the country in which they were acquired.

Braganza, April 28, 1813

Since the date of my last, with the exception of a journey to Miranda, I have been stationary in this city. The Lent season has been an uncommonly dull time; day after day we have had nothing but masses and religious processions. On the morning of the Festa dos Pasos, while I was in bed, the officers of the *Juiz de Fora* entered my room with a *"con liçenca Señor"*, and proceeded to embargo all the spiritual pictures with which my Jewish landlord had decorated the walls of his room. These were to swell the pageantry of the commemoration of our Saviour's passion. In the afternoon this solemn mockery began. The military being drawn up on each side of the street, a herald led the way, bearing a Roman standard with the letters S. P. Q. R. He was followed by a miserable-looking naked wretch, flogging himself with thongs of twisted leather*. Then came after him two more in as shameful a state of nudity, dragging massy chains which were riveted on their ankles. A fourth followed, walking backwards, holding a naked sword between his teeth, and smiting himself with the blades of another two, having one in each hand.

---

* Perhaps in this disgusting exhibition are to be found some remains of the old heresy of *flagellantism*, so common in Italy (its birth-place), Germany, and France, until put down by Gregory X. and the Emperor Rodolpho. This heresy, as is well known, consisted in the Flagellants maintaining fustigation to be more efficacious in obtaining pardon for sin than sacramental confession. These Flagellants were anciently very numerous in Castille, and obtained under the name of Bastajos.

Next came a cross of prodigious size, borne by four peni-tents, and followed by a supported figure in wax, represent-ing our Saviour. Behind him crept two naked wretches on all-fours, bedaubing themselves with the mud of the streets. Next came forward a number of children, gaily dressed out, powdered, frizzled, profusely painted, and having wings ap-pended to their shoulders. These represented angels, and preceded the *Gouvernador do Bispado*, who advanced be-neath a gorgeous canopy of silk, supported by two priests of inferior rank. The military governor, in a suit of sable, closed the procession, followed by the ecclesiastics of the town and a company of militia.

On Easter Monday the women are accustomed to as-semble in the streets, each bringing with her an earthen pan and a small stick. One of them is blindfolded, and being armed with a cudgel, tries to *"romper as panellas"*, which the rest of the party din about her ears. The con-sequence is, that not only a great many pans are broken, but a great many heads also, which of course adds consid-erably to the festivity of the occasion. In the afternoon, figures of men, stuffed with straw, and clothed in rags, are suspended in various parts of the town. These are all representatives of the traitor Judas; and after being heart-ily pelted and execrated by the boys during the day, are at night committed to the flames.

I am sorry to say that I have had a very severe attack of the *aguan* fever, and from which I am but slowly recover-ing. A very sensible old lady of my acquaintance always assigned as a reason for wishing to live, "that she might see what would come next"; and in my own case I must say, that it would be particularly disagreeable to die at present, as the army is just on the point of moving, and I have a great deal of curiosity to know what "will come next" in the ensuing campaign.

An order has just arrived from head-quarters, to form a very large depot at Braganza, which is to be the line of march for the second division and a great portion of the cavalry. We have also sent requisitions to the authorities of the different villages for a supply of transport, which is extremely scarce even in this province. The lowest rate of pay per diem, for a pair of bullocks, is four dollars. A labourer in the field earns half a dollar a-day (or twenty *vintins*), and a woman nine *vintins*.

May 14th. I now resume my letter, which I have been too ill lately to finish. I have been recommended to take a journey to Lisbon, and am in daily expectation of leave from head-quarters for that purpose. Every third day the fever attacks me, and leaves me so weak that I can scarcely sit on horseback.

A great many dragoon officers have already entered Braganza, to await the arrival of their respective regiments. The plan of future operations seems to be, that a part of our army will advance upon the Esla, and cross perhaps at Benavente.

General —— called upon me yesterday to look at some memorandums which I had taken of the villages between Miranda and Carvijales, which seems to favour this conjecture. He shewed me a statement which he had just received from a spy in Zamora, which sets forth the French force in that garrison as being 3,500 men; and probably this will be the first point of attack. A courier has this moment arrived, announcing the army to be in motion. The third and fourth divisions are to be at Vimioso and Outeiro on the 22nd and 23rd instant—the fifth and sixth divisions at Miranda de Duero, on the same day. Part of the cavalry under Colonels Ponsonby and Arnold will pass through this city. A nephew of General Castanos has just left us for Gallicia, to put the Spanish army in motion; so you may expect, before many weeks, to hear of a blow being struck somewhere. My leave has come; and I shall leave this in a day or two for Lisbon via Oporto.

Oporto, May 26, 1813

I left Braganza on the 20th instant, sleeping the first night at Val de Prados. On the following day between Bornes and Trinidade, I fell in with the right brigade of the third division which was marching on Vimioso. At Villa Flor you leave the Moncorvo road to the left, and descend upon the Duero by Carazedo. The country around Villa Flor is extremely wild and grand, and in its mountainous appearance much resembling that near Torre de Moncorvo. A remarkably high peak overhangs the town, upon the top of which is a chapel which has a pretty effect to the eye. The vineyards are pushed nearly to the summit of the mountains.

The descent from Carazedo to the Duero is by a frightful and precipitous track. For nearly two leagues no traces of men are to be seen, and some scanty withering shrubs are all the vegetation. After a forced march of twelve weary leagues, I reached St. Joao de Pesqueira, a town on the Beira side of the river, at a late hour. The route stood thus:

	Leagues
Val de Prados	5
Bornes	2
Trinidade	2
Villa Flor	2
Carazedo	3
Douro	2
Pesqueira	1

The next day I proceeded to Quinta d'Orgal, one league

from Pesqueira, and that for the purpose of embarking myself and cavalry in any barge that might be returning to Pezo de Regoa, a little town below Lamego. Although the *quinta* consists only of three or four houses, yet it is a place of first importance to our army at present. The immense business carried on here both by land and water transport is conducted with the greatest regularity, magazines being established at every convenient point for receiving and issuing supplies. The Duero here begins to lose its wild and gloomy aspect. It was late in the afternoon before I could embark. The evening sail on the Duero was delightful. We accomplished a distance of only two leagues, the navigation of this part of the river being dangerous by night, on account of the numerous rocks and shoals.

I landed at a beautiful little village on the right bank, and was hospitably received at the *quinta* of an old gentleman, who is one of the greatest vine growers in the district. I was regaled at supper with a bottle of the genuine juice, old and oily; my patron entertaining me the meanwhile with an account of the wine factory at Oporto. Its founder was the great Marquis de Pombal. Ardent in everything he undertook, this statesman was enlightened by a genius which never failed to direct his operations, and ensure their success. The better to induce the vine growers of the Duero to embark in this speculation, he commenced by instituting a bank which was engaged to pay nearly twelve per cent, for money deposited, the principal being sunk for twenty years.

For every 500 dollars which a proprietor of vineyards had in this fund, he was entitled to one *accaõ* (or dot). Ten of these *accaõs*, arising from the invested sum of 5,000 dollars, entitled him to one entire vote, whereas anything short of this sum only gave him the fraction of a vote. These votes were for the purpose of choosing inspectors and deputies of the factory. If any vine grower belonging to this company stood in need of a sum of money, not exceeding the actual value of his estate, the factory were bound to lend it, taking only three per cent, for the use.

The produce of the Duero and the demand for foreign consumption are both equally uncertain; but the merchants could generally guess pretty nearly the quantity they were likely to dispose of. We will say, for example, that they laid their calculation at 30,000 pipes for any given year. One inspector or taster of wines was then appointed by the factory, and another by the growers, to purchase this quantity from the proprietors of vineyards in a proportion regulated by the extent of their respective properties. These functionaries arriving on the Duero, find the produce of the year amounting to 60,000 pipes. What then could the proprietors do with the remaining 30,000, a quantity much greater than home consumption would require, and which, if suffered to remain in hand, would prejudice the vintage of the following year? To remedy this, the factory was bound to purchase one-third of the remainder, and to distil it into *agoa dente* on the spot.

Since the death of the Marquis, the greatest abuses have crept into the society, to the great oppression of the smaller proprietors of vineyards. In the district of Oporto, no one can sell wine for home consumption, which does not come immediately from the factory. In the society above described, every man who could command ten votes was eligible to the office of inspector or deputy, in which he was allowed to continue only two years. Every thing now is very different; a great many English merchants are possessed of large estates on the Duero, and the whole is a sad monopoly.

The wine at present is very cheap, being about 47½ dollars per pipe; whereas last year it exceeded twice that sum.

The death of the Marquis was followed by a general corruption in the whole economy of the Portuguese nation. In his time the standing army was 40,000 men, for the maintenance of which the people were liable to an assessment of one-tenth of their incomes; but such was the regulated economy of his age that they were never called upon for more than one-twentieth. The army at present, including militia, does not reach 80,000, and the inhabitants contribute nearly one-third of their incomes, the ecclesiastics being included, who formerly paid nothing. This, however, is easily accounted for when you come to learn that every tax filters through the not un-anointed hands of forty tax-gatherers, by which process the metal is supposed to fall more purified into the public exchequer.

I arose at daybreak, and found my old patron already stirring. He pointed out his vineyards rising in majesty above his beautiful *quinta*. The regularity of the vineyards upon spots so rugged and steep is truly surprising. The ridges rise one above the other in the exactest order. They have just concluded the first summer pruning, and are beginning to distil the *agoa dente* for the ensuing vintage. This part of the Duero yields the richest wine. It is almost black, and flows thick and smooth like oil. The body of it in its first year is quite surprising. The old man took me to visit his wine store cut out in the mountain and stocked with eleven vats; and with these eleven filled, he was accounted the richest proprietor on the Duero.

The store also contained the press and still for making the *agoa dente*, without a small proportion of which the wine would not keep to any age.

At five o'clock a.m. I re-embarked. The boat was filled with country people, as it was fair day at Regoa. The scenery of the lower Duero is truly enchanting; fine open Champaign hills studded with innumerable *quintas*, looking, as

Mr. Moore would say, like pearls in a sea of emeralds. The navigation of the river is, however, extremely difficult, and in many parts the current was so impetuous, that the boat was carried down with a frightful velocity. We were only an hour in reaching Regoa, a distance of four leagues! This last is a pretty little town, but almost choked at present with magazines and brigades of mules, &c. which are hourly arriving to receive their supplies.

On the following morning I reached Joe Longstaff's, in the Rua Nova, by breakfast-time, taking the same route which I described to you in my first letter from Almeida. I purpose staying in Oporto a few days to recruit, and shall let you hear from me again when I get to Coimbra.

Lisbon, June 10, 1813

On the evening of the 28th *ultimo* I started from Oporto, and slept in the convent of Augustin Friars at Grijo, three leagues forward on the Lisbon road. The friars are all *fidalgos*, nor can any under such rank be admitted into this fraternity. The convent is reputed one of the most ancient in the country, and encumbered with no less than 900 years of antiquity. The gardens and pleasure grounds which surround this venerable pile are tastefully laid out, and an aqueduct passes through them, bringing its water from a neighbouring mountain.

The following day's journey was a very pleasant one, the sea being constantly in sight, and the heat tempered by its breeze. The people of the Beira as you advance begin to look more swarthy than those of the Minho. The beggars on the road are extremely numerous and importunate. As soon as you approach any village, a troop of children nearly naked, and with mahogany coloured skins, scamper away before you, and compose themselves into suppliant attitudes beneath excavations of the high banks by which the road is generally confined, and then beseech your charity with every moving tone and gesture which misery and artifice can suggest. They invariably declare themselves to be helpless orphans, and, *"Oh, Señor, naõ tenho pay ni may"*, is the constant burthen of their lament, the parents all the while watching from their windows the success of this appeal to the traveller's charity.

The women of this province are very hardy and industrious, performing those agricultural labours which are usually deemed the province of men, such as sowing, mowing, guiding the plough, &c. In every part of the road you meet with *estalages*, tolerably commodious, but shamefully imposing. The traveller, however, must be content with fish and an omelette, as their larders afford no other kind of entertainment. I slept this night at Sardao, being one league from the bridge by which you cross the Vouga. The appearance of this river as you approach it is highly pleasing; winding and disappearing, and then disclosing itself again at irregular and unexpected intervals. Ancient geographers mention this Vouga as one of the chief rivers of Spain. Pliny calls it Vacca. Whatever it might have been formerly, it is at present unworthy of such distinction. No boats can come up farther than the bridge, which is distant only two leagues from Aveiro, at which place it discharges itself into the sea.

Were the Portuguese possessed only of a tithe of that public spirit which evinces itself in our own happy country by so many fine canals, and other public works, it would be easy to render this river navigable nearly to Vizeu, and so a running trade would be kept up between that city and Aveiro. The lower bridge of the Vouga, leading to Sardao, is of Roman structure, but is almost entirely obscured by the present one, which is built upon it. A branch of the Roman military road from Lisbon to Braga probably went over this, striking off at Agueda (Æminium) and rejoining at Feira the main road which passed through Aveiro (Talabrica). My reason for this conjecture is, that in several places I thought I discovered traces of that durable pavement of *silex* and *glarea* with which the causeways of this imperial people were generally constructed.

Sardao, or Agueda, is a large and busy town, or rather two towns joining each other. For a history of it, I have been referred to the works of Faria y Souza, a Portuguese, who wrote an account of his country in Spanish. This part of the province of Beira is extremely fertile, producing abundant crops of Indian corn, rye, and wheat. At Sardao the traveller loses sight of the sea. I left this place next day for Coimbra, distant six leagues.

As I entered the suburbs, the sun was gilding with its last rays the spires of this classic seat, and the Mondego seemed to glow beneath the rich dimness of approaching night. The streets were full of students, and well-dressed people of both sexes, who were enjoying the delicious coolness of the evening air, after a noon of most oppressive sultriness. I was too fatigued to be at the pains of procuring a billet (which would have required me to report myself to the British commandant, from whom I should have received an order upon the Portuguese magistrate), but took up my resting-place at the Estalage de Conde, a pretty good hotel in the market-place.

The university, which is now, in consequence of the war, but thinly attended by students, was founded originally at Lisbon, by King Dionysius (Dom Denis) in 1290, and afterwards transferred by him to Coimbra 1308. The students, before the French invasion, amounted to 1200; they are now reduced to 200. The monasteries here are very numerous and very rich. Massena, when advancing in 1810, had reserved Coimbra as a *bonne bouche* of plunder for his return. He was, however, unable to pass the Mondego, and Coimbra escaped untouched.

The monastery of St. Augustin is a sumptuous and spacious building. In the corridors are two or three tolerable, and a great many execrable daubs of paintings. The subject of one picture is a scriptural tree, on the ramifications of which are depicted the various religions prevailing in the world. In another picture, our Saviour is represented as an abbot, and the apostles as canons, with the inscription beneath of *"Apostoli fuerant Canonici, Abbate Christo."* On my return from this convent I was seized with one of the severest attacks of ague I have as yet experienced, and which left me in such a state of bodily and mental lassitude, that during three days I stayed here I never got farther than the banks of the river.

On the 4th instant I resumed my journey. At two leagues from Coimbra the traveller arrives at the once magnificent, but now desolate, town of Condeixa. That vengeance which Massena had reserved for Coimbra, fell with a dreadful fury upon this ill-fated place. The numerous palaces, which were once the pride and ornament of Condeixa, are now heaps of ruins. The conflagration continued during three days, and ended only when the flames could find nothing else to devour. I had always supposed Coimbra to have been the Roman Conimbriga, and it is noticed as such in several descriptions of this country. I find, however, that this distinction belongs to Condeixa, or that part of it called Condeixa Velha, where the remains of more than one aqueduct, and of other works of art, fully establish the point. Some have supposed Munda (an ancient city of Bœtica mentioned by Julius Cassar, and which has given name to the Mondego) to have been on the spot on which Coimbra now stands, but apparently without sufficient reason, since no vestiges of any ancient city have been discovered on the present site of Coimbra.

The termination of so many cities in *briga* has been accounted for, by referring their origin to a famous king of the name of Brigo or Briga, who gave his name to the cities which he built, and hence Conimbriga, Medobriga, Cerobriga, Netobriga, &c. It is, however, more probable, that this was a general name for city, in the old language of the country, and was added after some appellative, the same as the French added *dunum*, and hence Lugdunum, Augustodunum; or the Germans with their *burgh*, as Friburgh, Hamburgh, &c.

At three leagues' distance from Condeixa was Redinha, a populous and happy town, but now, thanks to the Gallic bands, a ruinous heap. It was my design to have stayed the night in this place, but not a habitable house was to be found. I slept at a miserable *estalage* half a league farther.

On the following day I passed through Pombal, distant five leagues from Redinha; a dozen houses or so are all which now remain. This town is commanded by a high hill, on which are the ruins of a castle. I visited the church, wherein are deposited the remains of the great Marquis de Pombal. The coffin is preserved in a neat chapel on the left hand side as you enter the church by the principal door; a black velvet curtain, richly ornamented with gold fringe, is hung before it. The French must have been strongly influenced by a sentiment of respect for the memory of departed excellence, to suffer his relics alone to be undisturbed, when the rest of the town was devoted to general plunder and conflagration.

The city of Leiria is in a very little better state than Pombal. Its situation—on the banks of a pretty stream—is delightful; and a Moorish castle in excellent preservation, and built on a commanding rock, seems to frown indignation on the ruins which lie beneath. Leiria was destroyed by Junot, in consequence of the people of the town having fired upon him when advancing on Lisbon. On this occasion seventy of the principal inhabitants were brought out and hanged.

In the evening I set out for St. Jorge, leaving the main road at about three miles from Leiria, for the purpose of visiting the celebrated convent of Batalha. Being situated in a hollow, the traveller is taken unexpectedly by the view of this once sumptuous and venerable pile, and which, even in its present state of ruin, conveys into the mind the loftiest impressions of all that is grand and beautiful. Every thing in Gothic architecture is abstract and mysterious. There seems in it an ideal charm, which gives rise to feelings of a high and inexpressible order. Here the eye wanders over cloisters, domes, pinnacles, and arches; in short, all that can delight the mind with a rich and lavish magnificence, and all that affect and overwhelm it with sorrow for its destruction. The mouldings of the columns which support the arches, are all undercut and grooved in the most exquisite manner, while the arches themselves vary alternately in their work-manship. One of these, as you enter from the cloister into the left hand aisle of the church, Buonaparte had directed Massena to take down and send to Paris as a triumphal arch. The *relievos* on it are the most beautiful I ever beheld.

An old sexton conducted us within the church, which is in a style of more simple grandeur than the rest of the edi-fice. The pillars and roof are quite plain. The altar piece is a choice specimen of most elaborate mosaic, and the arms of Portugal are represented on it. In the aisles are several very magnificent tombs; one of the Lancaster family, which intermarried with the royal race of Portugal in the 14th century*. By this time, however, it had become so dark, that I was unable to read the inscriptions. In the vestry, the old sexton, after devoutly crossing himself, opened a door, and shewed me, within a box, the precious remains of King John I., the founder of the monastery. I felt a strong and guilty desire to steal one of the royal hands, and actually had hold of it for the purpose of breaking it off from the carpal bone,

---

* Joaô I of Portugal married his son, afterwards Henry III., to Catherine, daughter of the Duke of Lancaster, in 1377. This, however, could not be the sepulchre of Catherine, as I find she was buried at the monastery of Popule-tum, in Tarraconia, by the side of her husband, who met his death by falling from a mule when hunting.

when the sexton, perceiving my intention, hastily returned the box to its place of deposit. The convent was formerly surmounted by a number of beautiful spires; there is now but one of the smaller kind standing, and which by appearance will not stand long. Batalha was partly destroyed by Junot—the completion was reserved for Massena.

For a circumstantial account of this convent (which is also mentioned by Camoens in the fourth canto), I have been referred to the History of St. Domingos (*"Particular do Regno do Portugal, Lib. VII."*), which I have had no opportunity of meeting with in Lisbon. Indeed books in this city seem to be as great rarities as in the times when they were written on linen and skins. It was called *"Real Convento da Nossa Senhora da Vittoria, no lugar da Batalha"*, and was founded by John I. of Portugal, after gaining a signal victory over John I. of Castille on the plains of Algeburota, near Leiria. The battle began near St. Jorge. The Portuguese force being greatly inferior in numbers, John bound himself by an oath, that if he gained the day, he would consecrate a most magnificent temple to the Goddess of Victory.

The Spaniards were defeated; and John, luring from all parts of Europe the most renowned architects by the promise of great rewards, commenced his grand undertaking. The fame of this temple soon spread throughout the world, and princes came from the most distant parts to do homage at its shrine. Emanuel Paleologo, Grand Señor of Constantinople, paid King John a visit here on his return from Paris, and enriched the convent with some costly jewels.

Between this and Lisbon there is little which merits description. My route lay through Rio Major and Alcoentra, and thence through Castanheira, a good town eight leagues from Lisbon, but much destroyed. Two leagues beyond this you come to Villa Franca, in which are a great many magnificent houses, chiefly belonging to Lisbon merchants, who have rebuilt or repaired them since the ravages of the French. Half a league beyond Villa Franca you arrive at the famous lines of Torres Vedras. The flats between the high road and the Tagus (which first appears in sight at Castanheira) were defended in part by numerous salt-pits; but Lord Wellington, to make every thing secure, had trees cut down and laid across every interval where it was practicable for troops to break in, while the high-road was intersected by a deep dyke strongly palisaded, and which you now pass by a wooden bridge.

On the right of the road, looking towards the capital, the country is mountainous, and continues so until you reach the sea. As soon as you cross the bridge, batteries begin to surprise you in every direction. These are constructed with logs of wood piled one upon another; and there is a chain of them from the Tagus to the coast. Alhandra and Alverca are two pretty towns, both situated on the banks of the river.

At Villa Franca, the traveller is delighted with the exuberant richness of nature, and which makes an impression so much the more pleasing, as the many barren spots and ruined towns between Coimbra and that place had occasioned very different sensations. From Villa Franca to Lisbon the country is one continued garden. Between Alverca and Sacavem you pass through an almost unbroken chain of villages, of which the most considerable is Povoa. I remarked that all these little places mock the great city. A narrow ascent up a stony hill, leading to an insignificant chapel is called Rua d'Egreja (Church Street). That which leads into an open space hardly large enough for a sheep-fold is the Rua de Praça. A crooked dirty lane is baptized Rua Direita (Direct Street).

At Sacavem I found great preparations making for a fair which was to be holden next day (Sunday). The toy and lemonade shops were already open, and the road thronged with people, hastening thither with their merchandize. An arm of the Tagus comes up to Sacavem, which you pass by a bridge of boats.

A pleasant ride of two leagues brought me into Lisbon, and I have lodgings in the Alcantara, at an hotel kept by one Luis Perez, a comfortable and well conducted house. Lord Waldegrave and his lady are under the same roof. The best streets in Lisbon are those called Ruas dos Ourives, chiefly inhabited by gold and silver smiths. These are spacious, and the houses are of white free-stone, built with great uniformity. The Exchange is a fine open square by the river side, admirably situated for the men of commerce. In the centre of this, is the much celebrated equestrian statue of Joaõ II.

Besides these places, with the exception of another street or two, the rest of the commercial parts of Lisbon, is on a par with Wapping or Thames Street. The filthiness of the numerous alleys and steep lanes is inconceivable, and were it not for those scavengers, the dogs, a pestilence would be in constant recurrence. So numerous is the canine race, that one would imagine Anubis to be the tutelary deity of the Lisbonites, as well as of the ancient Egyptians.

I shall not take up your time with a description of the Tagus, which you can have so much better from other sources, and for the same reason, you will not receive from me any farther detail respecting the city, which by no means answers the idea which the proud epithet *"Felicitas Augusta* "had raised in my mind. The poor honest Portuguese, with a laudable partiality, deem both their river and their city the finest in the world. On the road, when they heard I had not as yet been in Lisbon, they would cross themselves and exclaim *"Jesu Maria!* never at Lisbon!" Then would follow an eulogium upon its magnificence, although themselves, perhaps, had never seen it but once in their lives. At every village on the road, your host, if a degree beyond a peasant, will always regret that "he is not at Lisbon to entertain you." If you ask for any article not in general request, at any provincial shop, the answer is generally, *"Naõ Senhor, aqui no ha—a Lisboa muito."*

I was last night at the Italian Opera (Teatro de S. Carlos), which is really excellent, and affords a rich treat of "nonsense well tuned"; for Music, as in other parts of the world, enjoys a signal triumph over her fair sister, Poesy.

There is an incredible ignorance here respecting army movements. I heard at the Ambassador's party a few nights ago, that our troops had crossed the Ezla, and that the French had retired upon Palencia.

Santandero, 26 July, 1813

You will perceive that I have made a long journey since the date of my last, having traversed about 700 miles of country. I regret now that I did not write to you from Palencia or Valladolid, as what I shall have to say will swell this letter beyond all reasonable compass. A trader will sail from this for Plymouth in a few days, so I must lose no time in giving you, in the shortest manner, some detail of this long journey. I varied my journey through Portugal as much as possible, taking the route of Santarem, Thomar, and Castello Branco.

It was at Mirandella, in the Tras-os-Montes, that I learned the glorious news of the defeat of the French at Vittoria. The town was illuminated, and the joy of the Portuguese unbounded. Chaves, the *Aquæ Flaviæ* of the Romans, has still to boast of the magnificent bridge, built by Trajan over the Tamega, consisting originally of sixteen arches. At present only twelve remain.

At Carvijales, which I have before mentioned, I fell in with a troop of the German Legion, who were on their march to the army. I made an acquaintance with Baron ———, the commanding officer, and on the following day joined them on the route. As they had a quarter-master attached to them, I became thus relieved from the trouble of seeking billets for myself.

At a distance of two leagues from Carvijales we crossed

the Ezla, a requisition having been previously made for the use of the royal boats to transport the troop. The depth of the river where we crossed is nearly 100 feet, and exceedingly rapid. A little higher up, towards Benavente, at a place which is often fordable, four cavalry and fifteen infantry were drowned in the late advance. Two leagues on the other side of the Ezla stands Zamora, the appearance of which, at a little distance (especially to one accustomed to the dazzling whiteness of Portuguese towns), is not very striking, the houses being built of brick burnt to a deep brown colour. It is defended by a single wall, and that of no strength. The French, during the last winter, had built the gate by which we entered. This day was so excessively hot, 96° in the shade, that I was glad to retreat to my billet, which was ready at my arrival.

In the evening the Plaza was thronged with politicians, debating upon two different reports which had been brought in during the afternoon; the one, that a general engagement had taken place, and that we were in full retreat; the other, that head-quarters were at Tolosa. The first was the most credited; and from what I could learn, the most desired. Don Julian Sanchez, who was here with his guerrillas, had left the city the day before our arrival, upon a summons from Valladolid, which seemed to favour the opinion that we had met with some reverse of fortune.

Adjoining the Plaza is a tolerable square, disfigured by an hospital, very irregularly built, on one side of it, while on the other it is as much recommended by a beautiful little building, formerly a palace of the Duke de l'Infantado, but now appropriated as a receptacle for bastard children. On one side of the arched entrance is a turning box for the reception of the children, with a bell attached to it, which the party rings as a summons to the matron, called here the Madre Reitoria.

The bridge over the Duero, consisting of thirteen arches, was accounted a splendid piece of architecture, and to which its present remains bear ample testimony. It was blown up by us on the retreat from Burgos. The Duero presents a very different appearance to what it does in Portugal; its steep and rocky banks being here softened down into delicious meadows and open vineyards. The numerous convents on its banks have been all demolished by the French. The present inhabitants do not exceed 4,000 in number. It is a clean well regulated town; notices being affixed in various parts, describing where rubbish is to be laid, and threatening with a penalty of two *ducats* those who do not comply with the order, or who throw out any dirt from their windows. I wish the Portuguese would imitate this example. The inhabitants speak very highly of the conduct of the French during the period of their being quartered here. The women are quite enthusiastic in their commendations of them.

This city was anciently called Sertoria, probably from Sertorius, and was changed by the Moors to Zamora, or Medina de Zamorati, which in their language is said to mean "the Town of Turquoises." A considerable number of these stones having been found in the vicinity, seems to favour this account. That hero of romance, the famous Don Sancho, met his death in this city, as I find in an old piece of poetry—

En el real de Zamorar
Grandes alaridos dan
Por la muerte de Don Sancho,
Qui acabava de espirar.

The peasant women in this part are extremely fantastical in their style of dress. Their hair is neatly plaited, and tied up with various coloured ribbons, which hang down in

113

tails. Round their necks they wear gold chains, from which depend crosses or other holy trinkets, such as figures of certain saints or of the Virgin. These constitute the fair damsel's dowry, who is of great or moderate fortune, according to the size and splendour of her necklace; so that a swain has never any occasion to make those impertinent inquiries which fortune-hunters with us are obliged to do. An half shawl, generally red, and always bordered by a different colour, is thrown over her shoulders, and drawn in rather tight about the waist. The petticoat is yellow or red, but seldom of the same colour with the shawl, which if red, then the petticoat will be a bright yellow with a red border. It is reckoned very ornamental to stick out the stomach. Their legs are rather thick. Stockings blue, with brown clocks. Shoes large, and generally resplendent with a pair of silver buckles. So much for costume.

In person they are of middle size; eyes black and sparkling; teeth white and regular; and if I add that labour has given them the lustre of health, I think the picture will be complete. The description, however, in *toto*, only suits the peasant woman in her holiday attirements, when the dance calls her forth to the village green. The two dances of greatest note are, as you probably know, the *fandango* and the *bolera*.

In the former, the immobility of the Spanish features is truly ridiculous, while the movements themselves convey a meaning which appeals too strongly to the senses to allow of its being mistaken. Such a dance one may fancy among the voluptuous Ionians; but the rigid sons of Sparta would have condemned the *figurantes* to the black hole of Aristomenes. The fandango is introduced in better society with a little more decency; but from a specimen which I saw at Valladolid, its luxuriance will still bear pruning. The bolera is more boisterous in its lewdness, and may be characterized as a piece of four acts, in the progress of which, the passion it represents gains an increasing intensity, until in the last it becomes the ode of Sappho in pantomime.

It is three long leagues from Zamora to Toro; and the distance seems really twice as long, from the unvarying appearance of the country, which is here a continuous cornfield, in which the eye can find no mark or figure to repose on, and where the only idea excited is, "how the inhabitants can consume what they grow!" To add to the wearisomeness of such a march, you can never find a drop of water to slake your thirst, except in a village, and I began to sigh for the brooks and fountains of Portugal.

Approaching Toro, the costume of the peasantry varies. Upon asking some women, as we entered a village, why they all wore red stockings, while at Zamora they wore blue, the answer was, *"Es el stilo, Señor"*—(it is the fashion). There is something inexpressibly lively and prompt in the speech of Spanish women. Upon praising the legs of one of these village nymphs, she put her heels together, and drawing her garments tight around her, said, with a laughing air mingled with pride, *"Si, Señor, es verdade: son muy ricas"*; which literally translated, for your benefit, is "Yes, truly, they are rich legs".

It was nearly midnight when I arrived at Toro, not having left Zamora till towards evening, and having loitered an hour at a village on the road. As usual, however, in Spanish towns in the summer season, the inhabitants were either enjoying themselves in their balconies or in the Plaza. In this latter place were several groups of dancers, and parties of young men singing to the mellow and sweet accompaniment of the guitar. This instrument seems to me better calculated than any other to inspire poetry, except it be the harp; but you must not confound it with that *twangling* thing of wires which is often seen in England; the Spanish guitar is strung with catgut, and being struck with a quill, in imitation of the ancient plectrum, gives out a full and rich note. What Plato says in his laws respecting music and dancing, seems to be acted upon by the Spaniards, who consider them as the primary elements of education.

Music, however, is not cultivated with that extreme science, and view to effect, as among the Italians; but consists rather in the effusion of soft and plaintive airs, proceeding from minds imbued with harmony, and not studious of art. This taste for music they must have inherited from the Moors; for in those parts of Spain where this eastern people never obtained a footing, such as Gallicia and the Asturias, the taste for music is neither so general nor refined.

The *alcaldi* at Toro was just such a fellow as Horace describes in his journey to Brundusium, a pitiful, pettifogging attorney, assuming all the airs of the *intendant* of a province. I arrived next morning by breakfast-time at Villa de la Mota, four leagues from Toro, having eluded the noon-tide heat, by starting at break of day. As the cavalry route was by Medina de Rio Seco, I left them in the afternoon for Valladolid, with a promise to rejoin the party at Palencia. I slept at Tordesillas, founded by Sylla, the dictator, which being known, Tordesillas is easily resolved into its original appellation *"Turns Syllana."* In the same way, Pampeluna readily suggests itself to have been Pompeluna, as founded by Pompey the Great. Tordesillas is celebrated by the loves and fooleries of Queen Jane, surnamed the *"folle"*, mother of Charles V., who lived and died here.

The march from this place to Valladolid (six leagues) was truly delightful, the road lying by the banks of the Duero, which was constantly in sight, and the country presenting every variety of cultivation, such as orchards, vineyards, corn-fields, and meadows.. There is nothing like travelling on horseback, if you would enjoy a beautiful and picturesque country; the senses are kept wide awake; whereas in coaches, you travel as if only to arrive at the journey's end, and yawn or sleep over the stages; at least I generally do.

The peasantry in this part of Castille are fine representatives of the men of other times, as well in stature and strength as in courage and love of freedom. Pensive and taciturn, they are not easily opened out into familiarity; and there is a principle of pride within them that will not brook the imperious manner in which we had been so long accustomed to treat the Portuguese peasantry.

"Buenas dias, paysano!" said I to a countryman whom I was passing on the road.

"Tambien a usted, cavallero!" was the laconic reply—an emphasis being laid on the last word, as if to reproach me for the term peasant.

Had I said *"labrador"* (labourer), he would not have been affronted, since all who live in the *aldeas* or villages are termed indiscriminately *"labradores"*, to distinguish them from the inhabitants of towns or cities.

A little farther on, I overtook a muleteer driving his two beasts, laden with some kind of merchandize. Every now and then he broke out into a stanza from a patriotic song which I had often heard, the burthen of which is, that General Ballasteros had got a donkey, with which he was going to fetch Ferdinand out of France; and that a soldier of the House of Bourbon is worth all the regiments of Napoleon. The air, however, is extremely wild and original*.

---

* The words are:
El General Ballasteros tiene un borrico
Para sacar de la Francia el Rey Fernando.
La muger de Nigretté tiene un tintero
Para mojar la pluma de José Primeiro.
Mas vale un soldado de los de Bourbon
Que todos los regimientos de Napoleon.
Nigretté was governor of Pampeluna, and it is said his wife intrigued with Joseph Buonaparte.

His mules were fantastically decorated about the head with ornaments of plated metal and fur, and their tails were tied up with red and yellow ribbons. The hair from the shoulders to the hinder quarters was closely shaven off, except a little which had been preserved about the tail, and which, on the one mule, was disposed into the motto of *"Viva mi amo"*, (long live my master), and on the other, "Viva Fer^{db} S^{to} (long life to Ferdinand the VIIth). Clipping the hair of the mules from off the back is a very general practice, and is supposed, by keeping the parts cool, to prevent the *albardas* or pack saddles from hurting them.

I had left Tordesillas in such good time that nearly the whole day was before me in Valladolid*. The *alcaldi* was quite the reverse of his colleague in Toro, and gave me a billet upon a family, where I experienced an unusual instance of hospitality. They were nearly related, if I mistake not, to the Marquis de la Mota, and lived in the best style. The ladies were so agreeable, that I saw much less of the city and its buildings, than I otherwise should have done. In the evening I accompanied them to a *tertullia*, which was attended by all the fashion of the place.

I really think there is less of art in the composition of Spanish women than of any other people whatever. They neither paint nor patch, nor have those periodical moultings of feather which fashion elsewhere prescribes, but they all dress nearly alike, and in the same way at all seasons; so that Señora Maria is only to be distinguished from Señora Mariana, by a countenance more melancholy, by black eyes swimming in a more liquid whiteness, or by a figure (which is ever graceful) of a somewhat larger or smaller mould.

The *basquina*, or black silk petticoat, is generally bordered

* Valladolid was anciently called Pincia. It was a favourite place of residence with the Moors. Some fanciful etymologists have derived its flaire from Vallis Oleti; one Oleto, a Moor, being said to have been governor of the city.

at the bottom with black beads, and so disposed into an open kind of net work, as to afford the curious eye a casual felicity of admiring the most beautiful ankles in the world. Their stockings are of white silk, and they are never without a *mantela* (an ample veil of white lace), which is gracefully flung over their head and shoulders when they go abroad, and at other times adopted as a shawl. Small pieces of lead are attached, I understand, to the bottom of the *basquinas*, which accounts for the Ionian elegance of its foldings and fall.

Amidst the many changes that Spain has undergone, the women alone seem to be unchanged. Lattices, and jealousies, and *duennas*, and indeed all that used to give love-making such a romantic air in this, beyond that of any other country, have long since disappeared; but the passion itself still constitutes the existence of Spanish women. It is not, however, that intriguing kind of love which we hear of in France, where a lady changes her lover as easily and as often as her gloves, bat rather a devotion to one object, which renders them the greatest tyrants in the world, and makes them exact more adoration than was ever offered up at any idol's shrine.

I stole an hour or two the following morning, previous to setting off, and took a view of the exterior of some public buildings, such as the university, founded by Clement VI, the bishop's palace, and the remains of that where the kings of Spain formerly held their court; and ejaculating a vow that if ever fortune should lead me back to this fascinating city, I would explore it, even to the residence of the renowned Sangrado, I turned my back upon the pride of Old Castille, and pushed on at a canter for Palencia, in the kingdom of Leon*.

---

* Leon, anciently called "Sublancia", and also "Legio Septima Germanica", the city of this name having been founded by the soldiers of the 7th legion, in the time of Trajan. In old Spanish, the people of Leon were called Leoneses, and were perpetually at war with their neighbours, the Castilians, respecting the boundaries of the two provinces.

As I had the day before me and was unencumbered with any baggage, I turned off at Cigales instead of pursuing the direct road to Palencia through Duenas, for the purpose of seeing a grand specimen of Moorish magnificence at Ampudia. The town itself is inconsiderable, the inhabitants not exceeding 300, but the immense masses of stone which are still standing, and the extent of ground which they encircle, are living tongues proclaiming its former strength and population. Only a part of the castle now remains, but that is in the best state of preservation. Many of the chambers are astonishingly perfect considering the lapse of ages, and the little care and curiosity which the Spaniards evince with respect to early works of art. This place was perhaps called originally Alpudia, with the Arabic article prefixed.

Palencia is four leagues from this, and, owing to its low situation, you do not see it until on the point of entering the suburbs. It has a range of hills for the back ground, which our cavalry occupied during the late retreat. The city is situated on the banks of the Carrion, over which are two stone bridges at about 100 yards apart. Previous however to these the road is conducted over an excellent canal which connects Castille with the Asturias.

Palencia was putting on its gayest appearance as I entered, that is, the sun was setting, and the inhabitants pouring forth from their houses to enjoy the coolness of the evening in the public walks or ice-houses. I was billeted on a genteel family who were unanimous in their praise of the French officers. They had given, they said, quite a new character to their *tertullias*, by introducing the reading of works of literature as part of the amusement of the evening. I afterwards understood that the youngest senorita of the family had eloped with an officer of chasseurs previously to the battle of Vittoria.

As the cavalry had a halting day in this city, my Spanish host engaged me to dine with him. A large party assembled at two o'clock, and we immediately proceeded to the attack of an *olio*, a magnificent dish, and worthy of an *Archestratus*. In composition, it was, as you may say, rather heterogeneous. Beef and sausages, mutton and bacon cut into small pieces, sorrel and saffron, pigeons and pimento—all stewed together and disposed round a large turkey. Then for sauce, chopped chestnuts and shallots, cauliflowers and hard eggs boiled in butter. I fancy I hear you say that this mess outdoes that of the doctor in *Peregrine Pickle*; but if you will not take my word for its goodness, try it; and if not immediately registered in the family receipt-book, or published in the next edition of that valuable *"System of Domestic Cookery"*, I renounce for ever all pretensions to gastronomy. The white wine of Navarre (from the neighbourhood of Roncevalles) was excellent, and the red of Riocca only tolerable, as it flavoured most abominably of the skin. The Spaniards still use this primitive method of transporting their wine in *pellecos* (or sheep skins dressed with pitch). Two of these misshapen looking bottles when full are a mule load, and are much more easily carried than two barrels could be.

The only object worth seeing in Palencia is the cathedral, the interior of which is in a style of simple grandeur. The form of the building is that of an oblong spheroid, the aisles rounding off at the two extremities, and meeting in the vertex of a cone. There are some tolerable paintings in the little oratories which are in the left-hand aisle as you approach the altar. Before one of these oratories a placard is suspended, announcing that the Bishop of Palencia grants forty days' indulgence to all who shall pray devoutly at this altar. In the vestry they shew you an optical illusion. They have a small picture representing a fish, a vile daub; but when you look at it through a small hole in the wainscot, it appears a striking likeness of Charles V. The inhabitants of Palencia do not exceed 3000. The French carried away all the beauty of the place who were willing to follow their fortunes. In every city I find they are liked, and are hated only in the villages.

Joseph Buonaparte was reviewing his troops on the evening prior to our army entering on the following morning. They who dislike or pretend to dislike the French, have all the following nicknames for King Joseph: *el potrilla, el coloso de Rosas, el siete quartas, el tio Pepe* (uncle Pepy). Pepe, indeed, is the usual appellation; whence derived I cannot say. unless from the Greek, or from King Pepin*.

On the morning I left Palencia (being per Journal, 16th July), while waiting without the town until the troop should come up, I fell into conversation with a Spaniard, by asking him respecting some ruins which appeared at a little distance on two sugar-loaf-shaped hills in the direction of the Pisuerga river. On the one, he told me, was once a magnificent temple, dedicated to Jesus do Outeiro (Jesus of the Hill), which the French had destroyed; on the other, the remains were Moorish. The Spaniard and I becoming familiar, in consequence, as I think, of my praising the men of Castille, and their antipathy to *"los picoros"* (for he was a native of Salamanca), he related, with a peculiar immobility of feature, how snugly last year he had murdered a French officer. The Frenchman had come to his house during his absence, and proceeding to take some liberties with his wife, whom he found engaged in chopping sausages, she resented his behaviour, and struck him across the forehead with the instrument which she had in her hand. At this instant the husband entered, and taking out his knife,

---

* It is the usual Spanish and Italian diminutive for Joseph—Jose—Guiseppe— Pepe. I have seen it derived from *pepino.*, a sort of cucumber, and which from its plentifulness is used as a word of contempt. Hence the saying, *"No vale un pepino "* (not worth a cucumber). *"No darsele un pepino"* (not worth a rush).

gave him, as he said with an air of devilish satisfaction, five hundred stabs; and putting the body into a sack, carried it out during the night, and flung it into the Carrion. Much as I was shocked at the cold blooded ferocity with which he told his tale, I dissembled, and pronounced him "a good patriot." Pleased with the approbation he received, he went on to say, that a few months before that, he had been engaged with some others in throwing poison into the well of the barrack-yard, and that in consequence more than twenty soldiers were carried off.

It would have been idle labour to have attempted to subvert my doughty Castilian's notions as to the right of dispatching one's enemies by any means whatever. He had never heard of Grotius or Vattel; nor had he any idea that enemies should be considered as men like ourselves, whom, if we cannot subdue manfully by force of arms, we should be ashamed to destroy cowardly and at the expense of those charities which connect all mankind.

The march of this day presented us with a nearer view of the Asturian mountains. We were billeted for the night at Herrera, on the banks of the Pisuerga, and drew rations of the commissary there stationed. Aguilar do Campo, which was our next stage, we found a miserable town. The carriage of Joseph Buonaparte, which had been taken at Vittoria by the 10th hussars, was brought in here in the evening.

On the following morning we set out for Reynosa, in the Asturias, distant five leagues from Aguilar, the whole of which is a gradual ascent. You cross the Ebro at about half a league previous to entering the town, which is embosomed, as it were, in a circle of mountains. The air is reckoned highly salubrious, notwithstanding the torrents of rain which fall very frequently. It is a remarkably fine cattle country, every man being a breeder. Hay is here what corn is to the people of Castille.

As soon as we were established in our quarters, we made a party to visit the source of the Ebro, which rises about two miles from Reynosa. The source may be known by an old castle called Mantillas, which is built on a singularly projecting rock, from the base of which bubble out the drops of water which give rise to this noble river. Lower down the stream, about thirty yards from the base of the rock, are two contiguous wells, which the country people affirm to have been plumbed without discovering any bottom. We had nothing with us which could enable us to verify this assertion. Reynosa was formerly called Fontibile.

I took leave of my German friends at this place, and turned my horse's head in the direction of Santander, distant about ten leagues from Reynosa, and halted for the night at Cartes.

There is much of historic memory connected with this place; the vein is rich, but I had neither time nor means of opening it. There is a Moorish arched entrance at the farther end of the town towards Santander, which is in a high and beautiful state of preservation. Almost every stone which composes this arch has some peculiar mark on it, such as swords and other implements of warfare. A great many are inscribed with a character like our letter S fallen backwards. The *alcaldi* could give me no account of it, further than that the arch was Moorish, and that the inscriptions which are engraven on many parts, are Phoenician. A very lame history! nor am I antiquarian enough to make it better. I suspect, however, that the Goths were concerned in the erection, although it departs widely from what is usually called Gothic architecture. A reason I have for this conjecture is, that over one of the houses in the town there is a tablet in Gothic characters, which they say is an address to Fortune. On the other hand it is maintained, that neither Goths nor Moors ever entered this part of the country, the ancient Cantabria.

The latter people made several attempts, but were always repulsed by the invincible Pelagius, the reputed brother of Roderick the last of the Goths, who lived in the beginning of the eighth century, and whose prodigies of valour have been the theme of many a romantic story. The successors of Roderick were not called kings of the Goths, but kings of the Asturias; Pelagius being the first who assumed that title.

Spanish writers have exhausted all their ingenuity in finding parallels in history of this renowned and chivalrous personage. He has been compared to Rehoboam, to Pelopidas of Thebes, to Brutus, to Thrasybulus who expelled the Thirty. His son Tafila has been compared to Nimrod, as he was a mighty hunter, and was slain by a bear, which he pursued alone in the ardour of the chase. This again furnished a parallel to Adonis, and only requires us to suppose a bear and a boar the same animal. The symbol of the bear is very common over the doors of many old houses in this part of the country, and may be some allusion to this tradition.

I reached my port on the following day.

Santander, August 28, 1813

A packet from England arrived a few days ago, and is to be followed by others in regular succession, so in future direct your letters to this port. The novelty of the service here pleases me much, and I am continually cruising about among the vessels and ships of war in the harbour. I have just returned from Santona which the French still occupy. It lies about twelve leagues N.W. of Santander. The *Arrow* sloop of war blockades this little fortress by sea, and a ragamuffin Spanish army of nearly 5,000 men, badly clad and almost starving, by land. The Spanish troops are nominally well paid, but it nearly all goes in stoppages, so that the soldier never has a *quarto* in his pocket. They receive eleven *quartos** a day, a pair of shoes every fifteen months, and new clothing every thirty months. It is therefore not surprising that the poor fellows should be ragged, and have goatskin tied round their feet instead of shoes.

The commanding officer of this force sent an application to us a few days ago for provisions, describing the situation of the men under his command in very affecting terms; that they were nearly perishing for want of food, and that all the remonstrances which he had made to the deputation at Santander on this subject, had been treated with neglect. This statement, abstracting some-

---

* A *quarto* is four *maravedis*, and is worth about a halfpenny.

what from its high colouring, was in the main a faithful representation of their sufferings.

The Spanish authorities, before whom we laid their case, denied that they had the power of affording the required assistance, and had it not been for our commissariat, they must either have raised the blockade of Santona or have perished before its walls.

I cannot too plainly express my abomination of Spanish governments. Every petty town has a deputation or government of its own, subordinate indeed to the superior *junta* of the province, but very badly recognizing its authority. Such a deputation is of course existing in Santander, and being composed of the most wealthy inhabitants, may be termed a citizen aristocracy. The consequence thus resulting from the whole power of the kingdom being divided among a number of petty governments, is the attention of each towards its own proper interest, and a total neglect of the general interest. The want of connexion, therefore, which subsists between one province and another, and even between two neighbouring towns in the same province, may readily be deduced from so defective a system; so that if the French invade Castille, the Biscayans will not stir out of their mountains to afford any assistance, and the Castillian refuses to leave his plains for the same reason. Thus they suffer themselves to be broken up in detail, like the scattered sticks in the fable, because they have neither the sense nor spirit to discern that strength is the product of union.

No country ever needed a reform more than wretched Spain. For upwards of two centuries she has been cursed with such a system of councils as could produce only misfortune and anarchy. There are no less than nine supreme or royal councils for regulating her home and colonial departments. From such complicated machinery, where wheel works within wheel, where one intrigue circumvents another, what else but disorder could result? The Cortes had for long been the mere shadow of power until the late events restored its influence.

For a length of time prior to 1808, the kings of Spain had been accustomed to assemble them as a matter of form, and after addressing them with some unmeaning compliments, to dismiss them until another session. This neglect of the great council of the nation paved the way for a greater still; it assembled only upon the accession of a new king to the throne. The last time it thus met by royal edict, was in 1789. Gallicia has a separate Cortes; Biscay and Guipuscoa have theirs. There are about twenty-six provinces in Spain, over each of which presides an *intendant*. These officers prior to the king's deportation had such great authority, that they were more looked up to than Ferdinand himself, whom the people regarded only as a sort of old Bonze, shut up in the centre of his dominions, whom they were obliged to remember in their prayers, and whose name was well suited for verse; Fernando Septimo being incomparably smoother than Carlos.

The Roman law, with some exceptions, is the foundation of Spanish jurisprudence, the only laws which she can claim as her own, being those which are comprised in the codes promulgated by her ancient monarchs under the titles of the *"Ley de las siete partidas "*, *"el fuero juzgo"*, and "el fuero real." The criminal code is very defective, and one striking anomaly to an Englishman, who is accustomed to regard the prerogative of mercy as best invested in the sovereign, is a "minister of mercy and justice."

I am sorry that I cannot describe the Spanish character in very favourable terms. I had perhaps conceived too highly of them at first, drawing my ideas more from romances, where they are uniformly represented as noble and generous, than from the sober history of modern times. The Spaniards seem to have retained all the pride of their forefathers without the principles which supported it. Absorbed in themselves, they hate the idea of a foreigner, and only tolerate him so far as fear or interest prevails.

You frequently meet with impassioned feelings in favour of liberty in individual characters, but not that mass of feeling which you would expect from a multitude supposed to be animated with the same hatred to slavery. Those ebullitions of patriotism which seemed so fair and glorious in their commencement, have long since subsided, and the Spaniards, in becoming amateurs of slavery, unhappily realize that sentiment of Vauvergais, *"La servitude abaisse les hommes jusqu'à se faire aimer."* The cause of liberty in this country seems to have expired with the Marquis de Romana, and no one has since succeeded to him in the mixed character of true patriot and consummate general.

With the passions of an Englishman, I cannot but wish to see freedom triumphant all the world over; but it is a problem whether this country at present is fit for this blessing. The superstition, ignorance, and selfishness of the Spaniards must first begin to give way, before they can enjoy it in. a secure and permanent form. The deliverance of the Peninsula from French usurpation is an sera which is fast approaching; but whether this people will carry forward the schemes of national improvement, which the gigantic mind of Napoleon seems to have projected, or relapse into the darkness of the middle ages, must be left for time to decide. I do not either attempt or desire to justify the conduct of Napoleon towards this country, considering it in a human point of view, but I see no reason why we may not suppose him to be a scourge under Providence, to bring about a better order of things.

The people of Spain are not like some nations, fond of a little innovation now and then. On the contrary, they have an austere relish for old *mumpsimus,* and without some foreign impulse would continue to groan under an intolerable weight of priest-craft and oppression. It is a strange way certainly of dispelling the clouds of error, to introduce truth amongst men by the point of the bayonet; this looks like only destroying one tyranny by another. But as in the course of nature many things are necessary, which no one will admit to be desirable, such as hurricanes and tornadoes, so in political societies when they become corrupted and depraved.

The situation of Santander is well adapted for extensive commerce. An arm of the sea flows up about three miles inland. The harbour might easily be defended against the attacks of an enemy's fleet, the entrance being narrow in consequence of the protrusion of rocks on either side, and on which batteries were formerly erected. The channel widens after passing the entrance, and at its broadest part is about three miles across at high water. It is rather difficult of navigation, there being a chain of sand-banks on the left side, which extends for nearly a mile from the entrance of the harbour, while on the right, a little below the town, is a sunken rock. I do not suppose you ever intend to steer a vessel to this port, but I mention these circumstances with a view of shewing you the character of the people; when the French were here, buoys were placed upon the rock and sandbanks, but the Spaniards, as soon as they decamped, destroyed them all, in order to encourage their pilotage.

Santander is on the right bank of this channel as you enter from the sea, and ships of 400 tons burthen come up to the town, and discharge their cargoes abreast of a mole, handsomely built, and well furnished with stairs, cranes, and other conveniences for landing. The finest houses stand on this mole, and which thus completely shuts out the rest of the town from being seen from the water. Most of these houses are on a grand scale, being five or six stories high, and of a great depth. The lower parts are taken up as warehouses, the upper are the habitations of the wealthy merchants. In some, several families occupy the same house, each flat having a kitchen and other domestic conveniences.

The rest of the town consists of shops, which are chiefly taken up by Germans and Frenchmen, composing that mixed kind of population which is the usual character of sea-ports. The public market is well supplied, and affords provisions of all kinds at reasonable prices. Fish is in great plenty, but in no variety; that which is most common, and most esteemed by the Spaniards, is a long, thick, and coarse fish, with a black skin, and in its whole appearance monstrously ugly; it is called the *bonito**, and is an article of prodigious traffic; suffice it to say that you meet with it in the most central parts of Spain. It undergoes at the sea-ports the process of boiling, seasoning, and pickling, which is done with vinegar, red pepper and oil. It is then fit to be put into barrels, and brigades of mules carry it off into the inland provinces.

There is a neat cathedral, well hung as usual with pictures relating to miracles. One of these is pre-eminent in absurdity, being the representation of two decapitated saints, whose heads appear floating in a little boat on a most tempestuous sea. The story is, that suffering martyrdom by the axe, their heads were thrown into the sea, and sinking to the bottom, a stone took compassion on them, and being changed into a boat, brought them safe into this friendly port. I need scarcely say that this parody of the heathen stories of Orpheus and Arion is religiously believed by most of the inhabitants, and that a great fast

---

* It resembles the tunny, and is the *scomber pelamis* of Linnaeus.

is kept every year in commemoration of the event. A fast however, strictly speaking, becomes a feast; for although doomed to eat fish, which to them is really no mortification at all, the day always concludes with what is called a *Romaria*, a term peculiar to the Asturias, and which originally signified a pilgrimage to Rome.

It would be difficult to say who is the *arbiter deliciarum* here, yet everyone seems to know where the *Romaria* is to be, although these feasts are kept at various villages, and are occurring every two or three weeks. On the evening of a *Romaria* the town becomes nearly emptied of its inhabitants, who all repair to some certain village, where a grove of trees is generally to be found. Tables are arranged, and furnished with wine, lemonade, and cigars. Fiddlers and pipers are in numerous attendance, although select parties generally bring their music with them. Here you may see groups of young men and women, often the first families in the place, waltzing, or dancing the *bolera*: there a mixed multitude of peasantry and sailors and soldiers figuring away at the rustic *fandango*. This is the dance which has charms for me; in it you see sportive nature branching out into attitudes the most grotesque, and yet not inelegant. The peasant lads are arranged on one side, their fair partners, with long braided hair reaching to the waist, being opposite to them. Now they advance, snapping their fingers like *castanets* at each turn of the tune, then, looking languishingly upon each other, they pause a moment, recede, sidle, and turn round. The variety of costume in the men, the peculiar neatness of the women, with the graceful movements of their arms, finish the picture. In the dance you see the Spaniards under their most flattering character, for it costs them nothing to be gay. If they were half as jealous of their liberties as they are of their pleasures, they would be the freest people on earth.

It is a miserable thing that we can never know exactly what is doing in front, until we receive the information through the London papers. The fighting in the Pyrenees, somewhere about the Valley of Bastan and Pass of Roncevallos, has been, as we hear, unceasing and tremendous; quite a mountain warfare, consisting of a series of desultory attacks, the result of which is, that the French are driven back into their own country. St. Sebastian has not yet fallen. The courage and activity of the French Governor Rey is the theme of general admiration. Every manoeuvre usually practised at sieges has been tried on both sides, as well as some which are very unusual. An officer who came from thence wounded a few days ago, informed me that the shot of the breaching battery which plays against the curtain, pass over our troops at about two feet above their heads.

The Spaniards have fought better since the enemy have been driven over the Bidassoa, than they have ever done heretofore, and Lord Wellington seems to have more confidence in them. In England we say, such a one is going to pay the piper: the Spaniards, elate with the prospect of entering the fine plains of France, boast that the time is come for the French to pay *"la fiesta y el ajo"*, (the feast and garlic too).

I penetrated, about a fortnight since, some ten or twelve leagues into the Asturias, and had it in contemplation to push on to Oviedo, which may be considered as the present capital of this kingdom; Astorga, the ancient capital, being included within the kingdom of Leon. I was obliged however to relinquish my purpose, not being able to find any road that was practicable. The only method of reaching Oviedo from Santander is either to take ship for Gijon, or else to descend upon Leon, and fall in with the high road which leads through the Asturian mountains. The country

I passed through after leaving Santillana, the birthplace of Gil Bias, was the wildest imaginable, and inhabited by a race of men not less wild in their appearance, although hospitable to strangers. They were chiefly clothed with the skins of animals shot in their mountains. Their hair was closely shaven on the back part of their heads, but suffered to luxuriate about the temples. Their language was nearly unintelligible to me, from the guttural tone in which they spoke it. In short their whole appearance was original and striking, and made me think of that line of Lucan—*Hie prseter Latias acies erat impiger Astur**.

---

* Astur was the charioteer of Memnon, who, after the siege of Troy, came into Spain, and founded, as they say, Asturia, i.e. the present Astorga.

Vittoria, September 13, 1813

On the 1st instant we left Santander, in pursuance of an order Mr. —— had received from head-quarters, to settle the outstanding debts of the army on the late line of march between the Ebro and Vittoria. We took 50,000 dollars with us for this purpose, the carriage of which obliged us to make but short marches, so that we had every opportunity of viewing the country at leisure.

We quartered the first night at Torre de la Vega, four leagues from Santander. I was billeted in the house of a widow, whose husband and son had been both shot by the French, in cold blood, when they forced the passes of the Escudo Mountains under General Merle, and occupied Santander.

The peasantry of the country, under the command of the Bishop of Santander, gave the French the greatest annoyance, by cutting off their parties whenever they chanced to stray in search of provisions and forage. I asked a Spaniard whether the bishop ever fought hand to hand with *"los picoros"*?

He answered, "No; he only looked on, and preferred prayers for the success of his guerrillas."

This, methinks, was more episcopal than what is recorded of a certain Bishop of Beauvais, who always took the field armed with a hammer, so that he might only *"assommer"* the enemy, i.e. bruise them to death; by which tender conduct he avoided the sin of "irregularity", which he would have incurred had he used a sword, and shed blood. The bishop is now living at Santillana, the French having razed his palace in Santander to the ground, in revenge for his conduct towards them.

So obstinate and effectual was the resistance of a handful of peasantry in these mountains, which are about ten leagues from Santander, that the enemy were often obliged to employ two troops of cavalry to carry a despatch to Vittoria. The following is an extract from an intercepted letter from General Merle to the Lieutenant-general of division at Vittoria, which I read at the *alcaldi's* of this place, and describes the activity of these mountaineers:

Mon Cher General

Je ne sais plus oùu vous prendre; voila ma troisieme lettre; je desire qu'elle soit plus heureuse que les autres! Je vous envoye un officier avec une troupe de huzzards, car mes couriers ordinaires n'arrivent jamais, et sont massacrés sans doute par les brigands forcenés qui infestent ces montagnes.

An arm of the sea flows up as high as Torre de la Vega, and might easily be rendered navigable. It is called Torre, from an old tower which is still remaining. Previous to the war there was a large cotton manufactory established here, belonging to the Duke de l'Infantado. The manufacturers were chiefly English; and I was informed that an Englishman and his wife were yet living at a little farm without the town. The morning of our departure this little place was becoming literally crowded with country-people, who were pouring in to an annual fair. The *Paysego* women were in full force; and as I am so near that part of the country which gives birth to these rural divinities, it will be proper to send you some account of them.

From inhabiting the mountains of Pas, and some others contiguous to these in the Escudo chain, they take the name of *Paysegos*. It is only in the coldest parts of Spain, and chiefly in these mountains of the northern coasts, and in Gallicia, that they are able to churn butter. The mild temperature of the district, and the excellent pasturage with which it abounds, enables them to supply nearly one-sixth part of all Spain with this commodity. You meet with these carrier-women in Madrid, Segovia, and even Valentia and Andalusia. Their articles of traffic are not restricted to butter alone, but to salt fish, *Sardinias*, and the pickled *bonito* or tunny, which I mentioned in my last. Their dress generally consists of a yellow *spencer* and short petticoat of brown stuff, reaching no lower than the knee, and disclosing legs, which it would puzzle one to determine whether they were thickest at the calf or the ankle; and to set them off to still greater advantage, these nymphs of Pas endue them with blue or brown stockings, with splendid red or yellow clocks. Their shoes are often nothing but pieces of goatskin tied about the feet.

These women carry two baskets strapped behind them like a soldier's knapsack. The lower basket is in shape of a funnel, the point of which reaches nearly to their heels; on the top of this is placed an oblong basket, the ends of which protrude beyond their shoulders. These baskets when filled weigh four *arrobas*, equal to 128lbs.; and beneath this load the women walk, nearly bent double, at the rate of three miles an hour, and often make a day's journey of six or seven leagues.

So accustomed are they to this load, that they seem to travel as well with it as without it; for when they return with empty baskets, they make neither longer journeys nor walk at a quicker rate, but continue tramping along in the same curved position of body. I have met with women who certainly could not have seen fewer than sixty years, outstrip my horse in ascending a hill, and girls of ten or twelve years of age breaking in to the profession under a load which would soon tire a London porter. They travel in troops of thirty or forty, and you meet with them on all the high roads.

Leaving Torre de la Vega, you are no sooner out of one village than you prepare to enter another. The annexed extracts from my journal will answer all the purposes of a longer detail.

	League	
Torre de la Vega		
to Campo Sano	¼	
St. Jago	¼	
Cartes	¼	Which you enter by the Moorish arch described before, after having crossed a handsome stone bridge over the Besaia. Number of houses in Cartes, 140
Rio Corvo	¼	
Puente de Sallo		Bridge over the Besaia
Puente de Caldas	¼	
Las Caldas	¼	

This last place has a hot spring of pyrites and sulphur, its temperature being about 90°. On the hill above, is an almost uninhabited convent of Dominican friars. The road here narrows into a pass between the mountains, no more level space being left than is sufficient for the road and the river on the left.

In these mountains bears are occasionally shot, as well as a sort of lynx or tiger-cat, whose skins the shepherds convert into caps and doublets. This pass continues for half a league, and could be defended by a handful of resolute fellows against a little army.

	League	
From Las Caldas to Barros	½	60 houses
St. Mateo	¼	
Los Corales	¼	100 houses

Every house of respectability has the arms of the family, blended with those of Castille, carved in stone, and emblazoned over the door. This was part of the ancient Cantabria of which the inhabitants are not a little proud. They are said to have been called Cantabrians or Biscaini, from the ferocious courage they displayed in battle*.

We met on our route several brigades of mules laden with wool from Segovia and Soria. The mule appears to bear an immense load, each carrying a single sack which is bigger than the beast itself. The muleteers afford a specimen of a fine independent race of people; countenances peculiarly expressive, costume at once manly and striking, consisting of a jacket made of the chocolate-coloured cloth of Saragossa, a *corslet* of white sheep-skin, and a belt of black leather about six inches deep in which they carry a brace of pistols. A pouch for ball-cartridge depends from their shoulders, and they wear the large slouched hat peculiar to the Castillians. The peasantry of the Asturias wear high pointed caps made of thick cloth. We passed:

	League		
Samahos	¼	40 houses	Fine cultivation; rich
Las Traguas	¼	16 houses	pastures; Indian corn,
Arena	½	50 houses	and orchards
Moliedo	¼	70 houses	

At Moliedo we halted for the night; the soldiers who composed the money-guard being convalescents, and unable to make a longer march. We were quartered in the house of a proud, but not over-wealthy cavalier. It was in a manner castellated; and in the front and side-front there were embodied in the turrets six huge pieces of cannonry, which the owner affirmed to have been left here by Charles III.; but I should rather suspect them to have been taken from an old castle within half a mile of his house, of which some square towers,

* In the Cantabrian war, at the beginning of the reign of Octavianus Caesar, the women even of this province outvied each other in ferocity.

139

covered with ivy, are still remaining. The old cavalier had an only daughter, a pretty, interesting young girl, whom he had intended for a nun in the convent at Burgos; but the French had so plundered and destroyed his property, that he was unable to give with her the required dowry. Passed:

	League		
St. Martin	¾	50 houses	A little distance from
Barcena	¾	80 houses	Moliedo is an iron manufactory on the opposite bank of the Besaia.

The ascent was now becoming more toilsome, and the air considerably colder. The scenery on every side was magnificent—forms wild as chance could cast them. Some of the mountains, from the peculiar nature of their vast ridges, presented the imagination with pictures of lofty battlements and towers. Others again were uniformly gloomy, being covered with *gum cistus*, Cantabrian heath, and small oak. Here you may see the eagle on her nest, and there, a flock of goats, heedless of the gulf which gaped beneath, sporting on the very brink of precipices. The most agreeable odour of mountain flowers salutes the senses, while many a wild stream gushing from the rocks is ever ready to afford you a delicious draught. Leaving Barcena, we passed:

	League	
Ventoralla	1	
Nueve Fuentes	¼	
St. Jude	¼	
Besaia	¼	Source of the river of this name
Lansuelo	¼	Near this village, is a curiously carved stone pillar, considerably sunk into the ground. On it is a knight in full armour, holding a cross in his hand, and pressing another to his breast.
Reynosa	¾	

In my quarters at Reynosa, I discovered a little piece of antiquity in one of the supporters of the stair-case. It is the remains of a Roman pillar found on the banks of the river Ebro, at a town called Estriquejo (of which I can find no account in my map), in the year 1663, and dedicated to Constantine the Great. That part of the inscription which remains is as follows: Tino Pio Maximo. Victori. Semper. Avgvsto. And the epigraph above it is, *Juxta ripam fluminis Iberi ad eam partem qua tendit Juxta ad oppidum* Estriquejo—1663. Quære: May it not be read Est Riquejo, and this be some other imperfect inscription, not connected with the one to Constantine? The only authority for my saying what I have as to its being found on the banks of the Ebro, is that of the *escrivano* of the place, who could give me no other explanation on the subject.

There is a mountain one league from this, called the Arandilla Mountain, which can be seen from the sea, distant forty miles. We left Reynosa on the following morning for Villa Caya, and once more began to descend, which you must do any way you leave this place, as it is reckoned the highest ground in Spain. Our route lay through a pleasant valley, the mountains on our right hand rising in gentle acclivity, while those on the left were remarkably steep, and fringed, as it were, along the summit by a singular stripe of white looking rock or chalk, which appeared the more remarkable, as the rest was of a colour nearly approaching to black. This ridge resembled a chain of battlements built with the greatest regularity, and far outrunning the eye as to where it ended. We passed:

	League
Medianeros	1
Las Rosas	1
Llano	1

The valley still continued to present the same aspect, except that the white stripe on our left was gradually becoming deeper. The country here is highly fertile, and abounds in cattle.

Passing Theruelo, two leagues, we came to Soncillos, one league, where we halted. On the following day, at three quarters of a league from Soncillos, we began to descend a mountain covered with large oak and bellota*. Nothing which I have ever seen could compare with the magnificent spectacle on our left. The ridge of white rock became here swollen out into the most grand and gigantic forms. We were on the summit of a mountain looking down upon a valley, along the skirts of which, as far as the eye could reach, this line of barrier rose in perpendicular whiteness, breaking here and there into a *porta* or gap, of which the mouth might be a mile in diameter, and forming vast and regular amphitheatres, of the depth of three, four, or five miles, bounded on every side by the same white barrier. The appearance of this was magic itself, the light being reflected in such a dazzling blaze upon the plain of the amphitheatre, where the eye wandered over woods, villages, and streams, in the most enchanting diversity. As we descended, another and much larger *porta* presented itself, where we could look into a depth of prospect of nearly twenty miles, as far as we could guess, the rest of the interior space being lost in a blaze of whiteness.

The path we were descending was dreadfully rugged, and we were obliged to dismount and pick our way. When the artillery of our army passed here, it was a work of immense labour to get it down this mountain, there being, independent of its steepness, so many impediments from trees and rocks. The whole descent is about three miles. When we reached the level plain, we struck a little out of

---

* The evergreen oak. This word is pure Arabic.

the direct road, to inspect a natural curiosity in one of these *portas*, called *"Puente de Dey"* (or God's Bridge). It consists of one arch, formed by nature out of the white rock I have mentioned, and under which flows the river Nela. The span of the arch is about one hundred feet, and thirty feet in height, and is nearly a regular curve. We crossed this river five or six times in the course of the next two leagues, in consequence of its winding about the road.

At Villa Caya we came upon the flats of Castille, and bade *adieu* to the mountains of Asturia. This Villa Caya is a shocking dull place. Although it has to boast a number of excellent houses, and a large and well paved Plaza, the town itself seemed quite deserted.

I was so much taken up with attempting to give you some idea of the scenery on the left of our route, that I forgot to mention the distant view which we had of the Puente d'Arara on the right, where part of our army crossed the Ebro, and came unexpectedly in the rear of the French. The two capital movements of this campaign have been the passages of the Ezla and the Ebro; by the former; the enemy, who were expecting our advance by Salamanca, became compelled to retire behind the Ebro, with the purpose of keeping this river between us and themselves; but Lord Wellington, with consummate skill, despatched General Graham towards the source, who, crossing it at Puente d'Arara, turned the right of their line, and compelled them to fall back upon Vittoria.

We left Villa Caya on the morning of the 9th instant for Medina de Pomar, distant one league and a half. We had not proceeded far on our route, before we were overtaken by a Spaniard on horseback, with a bundle of receipts in his hand, for which he had come to claim payment in behalf of a neighbouring village. As he appeared a shrewd looking old fellow, with something inexpressibly sly in his countenance, we began to inquire who he was and what he had been. He informed us in reply to these questions, that he had been employed by Colonel Longa, the guerrilla chief, as a spy, and boasted that as long as the colonel lived he should never want bread. We learnt from him a number of particulars relative to Longa and his guerrillas, who had been quartered in this vicinity during last winter.

Longa, before the war broke out, was by trade a blacksmith and gunsmith, and excelled in it. Hostilities commencing, he raised a small band of *brigantes*, as they are termed, and armed them from his own manufactory. Ever since becoming a chieftain of guerrillas, he has occasionally resorted to his old trade, for the purpose of furnishing his men with arms. Some time ago he repaired to a village near Medina, and kindled his forge; when, as he was working away, begrimed with dirt and sweat, a small party of French unexpectedly appeared before the place, and thinking they beheld only a common blacksmith at his work, addressed themselves to a woman standing with her children before the door, and asked where Longa could be found, as they had heard he was in the village. The woman, with admirable presence of mind, replied, that she believed he was quartered a good way lower down, and named the house. Thither they repaired, and Longa effected his escape.

The French were not long in reappearing, having learnt from some traitorous rascal that the blacksmith they had seen was the guerrilla chief. They now proceeded once more to question the woman, and even the little children who were with her, but such was their devotion to his person, that they all denied having seen him. The soldiers making a search, soon found the unfinished arms, which had hastily been concealed among the ashes of the forge, and, as a shocking revenge for their disappointed hopes, bayoneted the poor woman and her family, and then set fire to her house.

When quartered last winter at Medina, an emissary was sent by the French to Longa, offering him 100,000 *reals* to betray his guerrillas into their hands. Longa affected to accede to the terms, but required 25,000 to be immediately paid down as earnest-money. The emissary produced the sum, which Longa no sooner received, than he had the fellow beheaded as a traitor; for he was a Spaniard. Longa gave his country another example of what is due to a wretch who would betray it.

Medina de Pomar was and still is much affected to the French. This Longa saw with patriotic concern, and watched his opportunity until he detected one of the chief inhabitants in treasonable correspondence. Upon this he had him seized, and trying him before a drum-head court-martial, by whom he was adjudged to die, ordered the magistrates of the adjoining villages to assemble the peasantry at Medina, on a certain day, for the purpose of witnessing his execution. The day arriving, he was brought out into the Plaza, where having his arms tied to the traces of two horses, and his legs to the traces of two other, the animals were driven off full speed at cardinal points, each tearing away a portion of his mangled carcase. A dreadful and revolting punishment, but well adapted to answer the purpose of deterring others from similar offences*. The old spy, whose name was Torre, related also many instances of Longa's generosity, which beguiled the way until we came to Medina.

Previous to entering this town, you once more cross the Nela, on the banks of which are the ruins of a castle which belonged to the Duke de Frias; it was destroyed by a party of Spaniards, in consequence of the duke, who is now residing in France, having given himself to the French interest.

* I am much inclined to doubt the accuracy of my own statement, and sincerely wish it may be incorrect. It is probable that he was hanged or shot in the first place, although at this distance of time I cannot charge my memory with the circumstance.

In consequence of the magistrates of the town stating to us that the army had done immense injury to the neighbourhood, during their late transit, we were induced to halt for the day, and examine the nature of their claims: these were found so weighty, that we got rid of a good many bags of dollars in discharging them. Medina has about 1,500 inhabitants; its situation is pretty, being built on a little ascent which overlooks the river.

We left it next morning, in company with old Torre the spy, and struck a little out of our road, to visit Salinas, where there is a large salt manufactory belonging to the crown. The pits cover a considerable extent of ground, and the channels and basins for receiving and conveying the salt water are well contrived. The water itself is supplied from a salt spring, and forced up by a wheel worked by mules. Seawater to this is as 9 to 20. They can manufacture 25,000 *funegas** yearly, and there is an invariable price for the *funega*, which is forty-one *reals*, out of which the crown pays the labourers sixty-seven *maravedis*. We passed:

	League	
Salinas	1	
Paresotas	2	Residence of old Torre, the spy.
Quincoces	2	
Subijana de Morillos	4	

At this last-mentioned place we took up quarters for the night, in the same house where Lord Wellington had stayed the day previous to the battle of Vittoria. At this point, you may say, the battle began; a large body of the enemy being posted on the heights which overlook the town, and separated from it by the little river Passo. Subijana is distant three leagues and a half from Vittoria. The skirmishing continued for several miles, till at length the light troops of the enemy fell back upon their main force. The track

* A funega is about 100lbs.

of the troops was plainly visible, especially wherever there had been cornfields, which were now all lying in the same direction, as if they had been purposely strewn so.

After leaving Nanclares, about one league in advance from Subijana, the hills on each side of the road suddenly recede, leaving the plain of Vittoria in the centre. We entered upon the plain by crossing a little river over the bridge of Puente Nueva, where the third division, under General Picton, passed. The seventh division had marched behind the range of hills on the left, with orders to debouche suddenly into the plain, for the purpose of carrying a bridge three miles in front of this Puente Nueva. General Hill, with Morillo's troops, occupied the heights on the right, having crossed the above-mentioned little river at Puente Roca, while the great body of the army kept the plain. The French, with an immense train of artillery, occupied a very commanding eminence at the extremity of the range of hills on the right; also a wood, which lies in the middle of the plain, and which they had filled with riflemen. Lord Dalhousie with the seventh division was not able to arrive at the time appointed for carrying the bridge, and Picton, aware that this was a decisive moment, attacked and carried it without any assistance.

The gallant general had been for some time under a cloud; the principal cause of which is stated to have been his rough and unpliant temper. The third division had always been called, *par excellence*, "the fighting division", being ever foremost where danger was the greatest. During the late advance, however, they had been saddled with the scaling ladders, and other necessary lumber of the army, and this had greatly annoyed Picton, and contributed to produce still greater ebullitions of temper, which it would have been more prudent in him to have restrained.

On the march, head-quarter's baggage has the privilege

of continuing its route, without turning aside to allow any troops to pass it. One day, Picton overtaking it with his division, ordered it off the road until he had marched by. A part complied, but Lord Wellington's butler refused to obey, pleading head-quarter privilege. Upon this, it is said that Picton struck him with the umbrella which he usually carried to defend his eyes, which were weak, from the sun, and accompanied his castigation with a threat of having him tied up and flogged by the provost-marshal, if he did not immediately give way to the division.

In the battle of Vittoria, Picton did not think that such a post was assigned to his troops as their oft-tried valour seemed to challenge. An aide-de-camp of Lord Wellington riding up to him shortly after the engagement was begun, and about the time Lord Dalhousie was expected to debouche, enquired of the General, " whether he had seen his Lordship?" Picton's voice was never very musical, and on this occasion it was absolutely hoarse.

"No, sir," was the reply, " I have not seen him— but have you any orders for me, sir?"

"None ", said the aide-de-camp.

"Then, pray sir, what *are* the orders you bring?"

"That as soon as Lord Dalhousie shall commence an attack upon that bridge, the fourth and sixth divisions are to support him."

Picton, drawing himself up and putting his arms akimbo, then said, "You may tell Lord Wellington from me, sir, that the third division, under my command, shall in less than ten minutes attack the bridge and *carry* it, and the fourth and sixth divisions may support if they choose!"

Upon this the gallant general mounted his horse, and putting himself at the head of his troops, waved his hat, and led them on to the charge with the bland compellations of "Come on ye rascals! Come on ye fighting villains!"

The bridge was carried in a few minutes.

These particulars I had from Colonel ——, who was badly wounded in the battle, and is at present laid up in Vittoria.

At a village in front of the bridge, called either Arinez or Gomacha, the —— regiment, under Major ——, lost, as Picton said, all the honours they had won. They would have been cut to pieces, had not the forty-second come up and relieved them. Major —— is reported to have been found skulking in an old house. Here it may be said the battle was gained, although the righting continued all along the high road to Vittoria. The houses in the villages, and the trees by the wayside, still bear testimony to the musket and cannon balls which were expended; while bones of men and horses, fragments of plates, pieces of wadding, old caps, relics of jackets, and cartouche-boxes, bits of rags, buttons, and shoes, are speaking mementos of this glorious and bloody day.

This victory, obtained with comparatively small loss on our side, has been the most useful as well as most signal one in the Peninsula. It is often the resource of ignorant generals to risk an engagement—when they are at a loss what to do, as Marshal Saxe observed, they fight a battle—but in the present instance, the French had their choice of either fighting or relinquishing the Peninsula; and so confident were they of victory, so secure in the fancied strength of their position, that even the probability of a defeat seems never to have occurred to their presumptuous minds.

The plunder on the field was immense. All the spoils of six long years of rapine became concentrated here. Even the wives and mistresses of the French officers were present in carriages and on horses, as though they had come out to see a review; and the scene which ensued when they found themselves deserted by the prestige of their fortune, and our cavalry dashing in amongst them for the purpose of taking tender charge of their persons and property, defies all description.

We found it impossible to obtain quarters in Vittoria, every house being filled with wounded officers. At length, after rambling about for two hours, I succeeded in hiring a little room in a dirty back street, by agreeing to pay a dollar *per diem*. As soon as I had taken possession of my cell, I walked out with a friend, in search of some place where we could dine together, and we soon made choice of a house, which a few weeks ago had doubtless been a *"Table d'hote"*, or *"Maison de manger"*; however, under the new regime, it proposed itself to the notice of the hungry traveller as being "A good English Eating-House". An English Eating-House in the heart of Spain!

We had scarcely entered, when a loquacious little Frenchwoman pulled us into the kitchen in order to choose our dinner. It was well furnished with comestibles: plenty of game, and more than plenty of pigs' feet and calves' ears. Our repast consisted of a *"bif-stek a l'Angloise"*, a bottle of English porter, English cheese, and two bottles of Bourdeaux, which from its flavour might have been English too. The bill, of course, must be English; and it was so, even to the fearful initials of £. s. d., under which you might read £2. 7s. 6d. or nine dollars and a half, as they passed for five shillings each. But then we were English—*"bons gens"*, as the Frenchwoman called us; and as this was a "good English eating-house", it was impossible to be otherwise than satisfied.

We closed our evening at the theatre, where we found the histrionic gentlemen ridiculing the French, having no doubt in our reverses done us a similar favour. Never were people less calculated for the sock than the Spaniards; they move about like monkeys taught to walk in slow time, preserving withal, even when they wish to be very facetious, a most provoking immobility of countenance, and destroying the sonorous flexibility of their language by the monotony of their delivery. The actresses are more engaged in looking out for winks from the boxes than attending to their characters, which consequently are no better supported on the stage than they are off it.

The night concluded with as miserable a pageant as ever disgraced a theatre. It was termed the *"Alliance of Spain and England"*, and the *dramatis personæ* will shew you that they can outdo Wall and Moonshine, and even those extraordinary personages, Strength and Force, in the Prometheus—

Espagna	La Industria
Inglatierra	El Rococijo (Joy)
El orgullo Frances (the	El Commercio
proud Frenchman)	
La Navegacion	Virtudes que no hab-
	lan (Mute Virtues)

This city abounds in billiard and gambling rooms, baths, *"maisons de cafe pour les officiers"*, and other *maisons* of a less reputable description; *"tailleurs de Paris"*, *"estaminets"*—in short, all the *friponerie* of the French capital in miniature, with more than a just proportion of its vices.

A Frenchman speaking to me of the morals of Vittoria, described it as a place well suited *"pour lacher la bride."* The women, taking them collectively, are supposed to be the finest in the world; and indeed it would be difficult to find a city where ugliness is so rare. Vittoria stands high, and a breeze constantly refreshing its streets, this may account for the women having such fine and delicate complexions. A great many of them have blue eyes, which you never see in other parts of Spain. There are about 12,000 inhabitants; its back streets, such as the Correria, Zepateria, are long and narrow; those in the centre of the town are broad and well paved. The Plaza is an exact square, being 140 feet each way. The houses in it are all built of stone of a dazzling whiteness, perfectly uniform, and with *piazzas* in front.

The park of artillery which we took from the French in the battle is disposed in three lines, according to their size, in a field in the suburbs. The French cannon, as well as the Spanish, have each a distinguishing name inscribed on them, such as *Liberte, Egalite, Fortune,* &c.

Colonel ———, who was wounded in the late action, will leave this in a few days for England, and has kindly offered to take charge of this letter. I will write to you from Bilbao, where we shall probably make some stay.

Bilbao, October 16, 1813

We remained several days in Vittoria after the date of my last letter, and then resumed our journey towards the coast. The country through which we passed, although extremely mountainous, displayed an enchanting fertility, being chequered, wherever cultivation was practicable, with vineyards, orchards, and cornfields. The wine, however, which is called here *chacoli*, is extremely thin; the fruit excellent, and in great variety. Peaches are the product of every garden, and are obtained without grafting. Farm-houses present themselves everywhere, and often surprise you in sequestered spots where you least expected to find them.

To speak, however, with becoming respect of this part of the country, the farm-houses should be called gentlemen's seats, for their owners, although they walk with long staves in their hands, often barefoot, and clad like rustics, and although you often surprise their daughters, like the beautiful Nausicaa, washing the family linen in the brook, assert, notwithstanding, their claim to be called *hidalgos conocidos*, or gentlemen of distinguished families. They are as accurate in their pedigrees as a Welsh genealogist, and sum up, with all imaginable ease, a long line of smoky ancestors as far removed as Pelagius. Some even will venture to strike as high as Tubal, nephew of Noah, who is said to have come into Spain 143 years after the Deluge, and to have founded, in compliment to his uncle, Noela in Gallicia, and Noega in Asturia.

The great boast of the Biscayan is, that he has no Moorish nor Jewish blood in his veins, and they proudly style themselves *"gente limpissima"*. Their language too, (the Basque,) is peculiar to themselves, having no analogy whatever to the present Spanish. This language existed before the arrival of the Romans, and was then unlike what was spoken in the other parts of the country. It is mentioned, I am told, by Pomponius Mela and L. Seneca, who were themselves Spaniards; the first being a native of Andalusia, the last of Cordova: the Biscayans assert that the same language is spoken at the present day, without any material corruption. It is reckoned extremely difficult; the curate of a village, who was a native of Salamanca, told me that it cost him the labour of seven years to acquire it. To unaccustomed ears it sounds a coarse and barbarous tongue, but is pronounced to be very expressive and highly figurative by those who understand it. The following words, which I picked up in my late peregrination, will shew you how much this language differs from Spanish.

Basque	Spanish	Basque	Spanish
Obeje	Pan	Episcovade	pouco
Adoaa	vino	Skarriscatzo!	gratias!
Suja	lumbre	A tos	veni-ca
Arraiwa	maldito!	Maneshu	chica
Vay	si	Es	no
Tshu	toma		

You enter the town of Bilbao from the Vittoria side (from which it is distant ten leagues) by a long unconnected street, which terminates in the market-place. This last is close by the banks of the river, over which is a bridge of one large arch nearly rectangular, consequently it is very steep and inconvenient for passage. At the left-hand side of the market-place, looking towards the river, is a handsome church, and adjoining this is the *junta* house, the lower part of which the merchants use as an exchange, while the apartments above are appropriated to the offices of the deputation of the consulate, of the *alcaldi*, and of the two deputies who govern the *señoria* or domain of Biscay; for the king of Spain is not king of this province, but only *señor*.

Bilbao, although so populous and of such commercial notoriety, is yet but a town; the natives, indeed, regard it as the capital of their republic, but the city capital is Guernica, an insignificant place five leagues from this, but whither the deputies are obliged to repair in order to their being duly elected. The *señoria* of Biscay may well be termed a republic, although it has virtually lost this distinction since the late revolution. Anterior, however, to this event, it paid little or no respect to the authority of the king, who collected no royal rents whatever in this part of the kingdom. The inhabitants taxed themselves, and after subtracting what was necessary for the public expenses of their *señoria*, presented the remainder as a donation to the king.

The only functionary allowed to act here on the king's account was a single officer of customs, for the purpose of preventing contraband trade; and it can easily be conceived what a shadow of authority he enjoyed in such office. The only municipal duties prior to the late events were a half per cent, to the consulate upon imported goods, and a trifling tax to the deputies for the *"gastas de la villa"*. The duties paid now to the consulate are become augmented to eight per cent. The Biscayans are so jealous of their privileges, that they will not allow any foreign merchant to establish himself within their *señoria*, and very few indeed from the other provinces of Spain.

The principal commercial streets of Bilbao run nearly parallel to each other, and terminate in the market-place. These are all neatly paved with small pebble-stones, and furnished with drains. Previous to the French occupation, no wheeled carriages of any description were suffered in the streets, but only a sort of sledge for conveying merchandise. At that end of the town in opposite direction from the market-place, there is a public walk by the riverside, well planted with trees, and in this walk the streets which are not commercial terminate. In these, many of the houses are of a sumptuous description, and faced with fine polished marble, while others are painted in a kind of fresco. In the Calle d'Estoufa, which takes the form of a crescent, the houses are all built of free-stone.

The population is estimated at 11,000, and divided amongst five parishes, with a church to each. Besides these, there is a tutelary chapel on a hill overlooking the town, dedicated to *Nossa Señora de Begonia*. By all accounts "Our Lady of Begonia" is a very extraordinary personage, having performed as many miracles as fill a folio. This folio is actually in print, and abounds with such tales as the following—An adventurous mariner of Deba, who was whale fishing off the coast of Greenland, seeing his ship on the point of being crushed to pieces between two enormous ice-bergs, prayed fervently to *Nossa Senora de Begonia*, and the ship was safely wafted *under water* into the harbour of Bilbao.

The priests tell the people that the sacred image of Our Lady, which is preserved in the chapel, was found one day near the spot sitting upon a thorn-bush, and from that time, which is immemorial, they built her a house.

Before the revolution Bilbao could boast of many magnificent monasteries. The French, however, sent off all the monks prisoners to France, and the monasteries are now converted into general hospitals.

I have taken frequent rambles into the mountains since I came here, for the purpose of observing the manners of the peasantry, who are extremely interesting, as being an aboriginal race. It is impossible for a stranger to dive minutely into their characters and mode of thinking, because a knowledge of their strange language is essentially necessary to do this, and they themselves speak little or no Spanish. The truest resemblance which I can find for a Biscayan mountaineer is, to compare him with the peasantry of Ireland. He is generally tall, nervous, and well made, with a most serious, and often pitiful, cast of countenance. In complexion he is white, with eyes penetrating, and nose aquiline. The crown of his head is often closely shaven, while a profusion of long lank hair hangs down his shoulders. They are very choleric, and I think treacherous; but they have the character of being extremely honest when once attached. The hovels of the lower orders are like those of the Irish; pigs and the family dwelling together, and filled with smoke. The generosity and hospitality of the Irish is however wanting, and a stranger is always considered by them in the light of an intruder.

We have some very pleasant society here; the *tertullias* or routes are well attended, and I have been fortunate in meeting with some young Spaniards who have more taste for literature than what the youth of this country generally evince. I am indebted to them for an acquaintance with the beautiful little *Fables of Uriarte*, the only writer of any reputation who has appeared in Spain for some years. I have not read his comedies, but intend procuring them at the first opportunity. His poem, entitled *"La Musica"*, is a very fine composition, which I would recommend to your perusal, and I should think you may procure it of any of the foreign booksellers in London. It was published at Madrid in 1784. Nothing appears to have been written since his day which will repay the trouble of perusing; and, indeed, in the literary as well as in the political world of the Peninsula, there is a miserable dearth of what Sir William Jones, in his *Alcaean Ode*, terms "men, high-minded men."

Most countries, under circumstances similar to those which have befallen Spain and Portugal, have put forth some commanding characters who seemed designed by nature to make a figure in eventful times; but here, with the exception of a few instances of middle-rate talent and bravery, all has been uniformly cold and barren.

Bilbao is said to be the ancient Flaviobriga; but it is likely that Portugaletto, a little town at the mouth of the river, is the site of the city of that name. The river itself is known to few of the inhabitants by any other name than the river of Bilbao; its proper name, however, is the Ibal-saibal, a compound Biscayan word, of which I have yet to discover the meaning. The present Bilbao was built, they say, by Don Sanchez in 1800.

Bullfights, which are now prohibited by law in the other parts of Spain, are yet tolerated in the republic of Biscay. There has been one exhibition of this kind since our arrival; but instead of those noble and daring cavaliers who used to enter the lists, we had nothing but a few butchers and blackguards. Even the bull seemed a degenerated beast, and required to be made savage with squibs and gunpowder; while the horses on which the *picadors*, or lance men, rode, were of that description called dog-horses.

Ustaritz, December 8, 1813

By the present letter you will learn that I have at length set foot on French soil. Our march from Bilbao, which we left on the 24th *ultimo*, affords but scanty materials for a letter. It was performed in haste, and under the annoyance of an unceasing course of bad weather.

Durango, five leagues from Bilbao, is a clean and populous town, much celebrated for its manufactory of gun-barrels. The best kind of these are made out of old horse and mule shoes, and so welded that nearly twice the weight of the iron in each barrel is lost in the operation. The price varies from six to twenty dollars the barrel; but those which are of the fabric of one Nicholas Biz, who lived about a century ago, will often fetch 150 dollars.

We quartered the first night at El-Orio, the appearance of which reminded me of a college. The houses are extremely good, and almost everyone has the arms of the family emblazoned over the door, and are inhabited by individuals who follow no trade. In fact I did not see a single shop in the place, and the grass was growing in the streets. Although every thing seemed so stagnant, it was nevertheless far from being dull, and I think it the most sociable little place I have seen in the Peninsula.

In the evening I had my choice of two *tertullias*, one a ladies' party, the other a sort of club, where the men meet to

discuss the gazettes and pamphlets of the day over chocolate and cigars. Like a good politician, I attended both.

In every town of Spain, however small, there is always a
patriotic club. In these meetings the usual taciturnity of the
Spaniard gives way, and he becomes loquacious, and often
clamorous and angry, if he meet with contradiction. He
tells you what his sentiments are with a warmth and energy
of expression which seem to imply—"be it at your peril to
think otherwise than I do."

The gazette of the evening contained the news of the al-
lied monarchs having made their solemn entry into Leipzig
on the 19th *ultimo*, so that now there is every prospect of a
closing scene to this eventful tragedy.

Our next stage was Tolosa, a fine old town, considered
the capital of Guipuscoa, and situated in the centre of a
beautiful and picturesque country. The peasantry here have
a method of turning up the soil which I have nowhere else
seen or heard of. The instrument of husbandry to which
I allude, is a fork consisting of two prongs, in figure and
proportion like a small *h*, the handle being about one-half
longer than the prong. Each man or woman is furnished
with two of these implements, and standing generally three
a-breast, force them into the soil at the same time, and
leaning back, tear up a ridge of land as effectually as the
plough would have done: a fourth person follows with a
hoe, whose business it is to break the clods. The scarcity of
cattle in this part of Spain has no doubt put them upon this
invention; but they are, however, enabled by it to cultivate
spots where no oxen could have ploughed.

After leaving Irun, a dirty hole, and thronged, at the time
we passed through it, with Spanish troops, you descend almost immediately upon the Bidassoa, the boundary between
France and Spain. The Pyrenees here are only gentle hills;
nor do they begin to erect themselves into mountains until

you approach Lesaca. We crossed by a pontoon bridge, and set foot upon the fine high road which leads to Bayonne. After a league and a half, we came to Urogne, which was totally deserted by its inhabitants, and filled with our cavalry.

We here enquired of some officers respecting the probability of our being able to obtain quarters in St. Jean de Luz, when they all gave it as their opinion, that, considering the approach of evening, it would be impossible. We immediately upon this prepared to take possession of some empty house by the roadside. It was only to choose between a chateau or a cottage, and we decided for the latter, as being more easily fortified against intruders. They all stood most hospitably open, exhibiting a miserable absence of doors and window-frames, which had long since been condemned for fuel.

At St. Jean de Luz I received intimation of being appointed to the staff of Marshal Beresford, and immediately set off for his headquarters at this place, a little town three leagues from St. Jean de Luz, and beneath the Pyrenees.

I have a miserable garret for a quarter at present, but I have an order from the quarter-master-general to take possession of a comfortable cottage adjoining the Marshal's garden, which will be vacant in a few days.

The river Neve separates us from the French, whom I see every morning at parade from the window of my garret. Our sentries and theirs can talk to each other with perfect ease; no kind of molestation being offered on either side. They come down to water their horses, and their women to wash the linen of the regiments, and we do the same. The French soldiers often endeavour to entice our fellows to desert, by sticking a piece of beef on the point of a bayonet, or by holding out a canteen, accompanying their action with "I say, come here! Here is ver good ros-bif; here is ver good brandy."

I was much amused a few days ago with the contrasted appearance of a French and English sentinel. The centre part of the bridge over the Neve has been blown up, but the abutments on each side are still remaining. On the one you saw the French sentry with his long musket, white cap, and loose grey great-coat, slovenly thrown over his shoulders; on the other, a Highlander of the 42d regiment, in all the pomp of his national costume. They were not more than twenty yards asunder.

The want of forage is severely felt by all parties. Our horses would starve, were it not for the furze-bushes; and even to obtain these, it is necessary to seek them at two leagues' distance; all being eaten up round this. Every other morning my Portuguese groom goes into the woods to forage, and returns with two mule-loads of furze. It is then necessary to pound it, which is a very troublesome operation; yet without doing this, the horses refuse it. All kinds of necessaries are equally scarce, and we are obliged to pay an exorbitant price to obtain them. Every rush light costs a shilling, and I use three every night, one in the stable and two in my garret. A small loaf of bread (2lbs.) two shillings; a pound of butter, four shillings; and everything else in like proportion. The rations for a common soldier *per diem*, consisting of 1½lb. of bread, 1lb. of beef, and $1/_3$rd pint of rum, does not cost the Government less than six shillings; perhaps even more; since the mortality which befalls the cattle between this and the Ebro is so great, that out of a consignment which I received the other day from Palencia, and which consisted, at the commencement of the march, of 500 head, only 180 reached me; the rest had died by the way.

December 11th. About six o'clock yesterday morning I was awakened by a train of artillery passing my quarters, and which seemed to indicate that some immediate movement was in contemplation. I hastily got a cup of coffee;

but before I had time to reach the river, the picquets had commenced firing, and our light troops had already driven back the enemy's skirmishers. The engineers laid down the pontoon bridge with admirable expedition, and I passed over it in the rear of the third division about nine o'clock. The French shewed themselves in good force several times on the heights, but always retired in a few minutes, leaving skirmishers to contend with our light troops.

At ten o'clock a heavy firing commenced upon our left, and became, as the fog dispersed, distinctly visible. The first division soon became warmly engaged, when the intention of Lord Wellington was, that it should only have made a demonstration. The third division remaining under arms on the heights which we had first gained on ascending from the Neve, I went forward with the sixth division. In a little time it was understood upon the field that General Hill had succeeded in turning the enemy's left. This was at about twelve o'clock.

A pause now ensued, the sixth division standing to their arms. I took this opportunity to enter a peasant's cottage by the roadside. A little boy was the only member of the family who could speak any French; the rest, consisting of an old woman, some girls, and two aged men, spoke nothing but the Basque, which is nearly the same as that which is used In Biscay. Their joy was so unbounded at the partial defeat which their countrymen had already sustained, that they capered about the room like a parcel of merry Andrews. One of the aged men impersonated a French soldier, and with an agility beyond his years, ran a few yards from the door, in order to convey the idea of a flying enemy; then distending his cheeks, he discharged a *bomb!* and fell on the ground, as if he had been killed by a ball.

The French now began to retire from a hill which they had occupied as a centre during the morning, and the sixth division immediately took possession of it. From this point we had a distinct view of the contest which was going forwards at about 600 yards in front of us. The object on our side was to get possession of the village of Ville Franche, which was obstinately defended by a force of nearly 3000 men. At three o'clock Lord Wellington and his staff arrived on the hill, and some light companies of the sixth division, supported by a regiment of *Cacadores*, were immediately ordered to attack it. The fighting now became very desperate; our men and the French being nearly muzzle to muzzle.

The enemy were at length driven out of their position; which was announced to us on the opposite hill, by a British soldier ascending to the top of a kind of cross which overlooked the village, and waving his cap in token of victory. I saw my cousin, Captain ——, go gallantly into action at the head of his company, and, I am happy to add, he has escaped unhurt.

LEONAUR

ALSO FROM LEONAUR

AVAILABLE IN SOFTCOVER OR HARDCOVER WITH DUST JACKET

THE COMPLEAT RIFLEMAN HARRIS *by Benjamin Harris as told to & transcribed by Captain Henry Curling*—The adventures of a soldier of the 95th (Rifles) during the Peninsular Campaign of the Napoleonic Wars

WITH WELLINGTON'S LIGHT CAVALRY *by William Tomkinson*—The Experiences of an officer of the 16th Light Dragoons in the Peninsular and Waterloo campaigns of the Napoleonic Wars.

SERGEANT BOURGOGNE *by Adrien Bourgogne*—With Napoleon's Imperial Guard in the Russian Campaign and on the Retreat from Moscow 1812 - 13.

SWORDS OF HONOUR *by Henry Newbolt & Stanley L. Wood*—The Careers of Six Outstanding Officers from the Napoleonic Wars, the Wars for India and the American Civil War, with dozens of illustrations by Stanley L. Wood.

SURTEES OF THE RIFLES *by William Surtees*—A Soldier of the 95th (Rifles) in the Peninsular campaign of the Napoleonic Wars.

ENSIGN BELL IN THE PENINSULAR WAR *by George Bell*—The Experiences of a young British Soldier of the 34th Regiment 'The Cumberland Gentlemen' in the Napoleonic wars.

HUSSAR IN WINTER *by Alexander Gordon*—A British Cavalry Officer during the retreat to Corunna in the Peninsular campaign of the Napoleonic Wars.

NAPOLEONIC WAR STORIES *by Sir Arthur Quiller-Couch*—Tales of soldiers, spies, battles & sieges from the Peninsular & Waterloo campaingns.

JOURNALS OF ROBERT ROGERS OF THE RANGERS *by Robert Rogers*—The exploits of Rogers & the Rangers in his own words during 1755-1761 in the French & Indian War.

KERSHAW'S BRIGADE VOLUME 1 *by D. Augustus Dickert*—Manassas, Seven Pines, Sharpsburg (Antietam), Fredricksburg, Chancellorsville, Gettysburg, Chickamauga, Chattanooga, Fort Sanders & Bean Station..

KERSHAW'S BRIGADE VOLUME 2 *by D. Augustus Dickert*—At the wilderness, Cold Harbour, Petersburg, The Shenandoah Valley and Cedar Creek.

A TIGER ON HORSEBACK *by L. March Phillips*—The Experiences of a Trooper & Officer of Rimington's Guides - The Tigers - during the Anglo-Boer war 1899 - 1902.